curriculum
connections

D1529451

Native North Americans

Warfare, Economy, and Technology

BROWN
BEAR
BOOKS

Published by Brown Bear Books Limited

An imprint of:
The Brown Reference Group Ltd
68 Topstone Road
Redding
Connecticut 06896
USA
www.brownreference.com

© 2009 The Brown Reference Group Ltd

ISBN: 978-1-933834-80-1

Editorial Director: Lindsey Lowe
Senior Managing Editor: Tim Cooke
Managing Editor: Laura Durman
Editor: Helen Dwyer
Designer: Barry Dwyer

Library of Congress Cataloging-in-Publication Data available upon request

Contents

Introduction

Native North Americans forms part of the Curriculum Connections project. The six volumes of the set cover all aspects of the history and culture of native peoples in what are now the United States and Canada. Each volume covers a particular aspect of Native American life: Peoples of the East, Southeast, and Plains; Peoples of the Southwest, West, and North; Arts, Society, and Religion; History; Personalities and Places; and Warfare, Economy, and Technology.

About this set

Each volume in *Native North Americans* features a series of articles arranged in A–Z order. The articles are all listed in the contents pages of each book, and can also be located through the indexes.

Each illustrated article provides a concise but accurate summary of its subject, accompanied where relevant by informative maps. Articles about major tribes are each accompanied by a fact file that provides a summary of essential information.

Within each article, two key aids to learning are located in sidebars in the margins of each page:

Curriculum Context sidebars indicate that a subject has particular relevance to state and national American history guidelines and curricula. They highlight essential information or suggest useful ways for students to include a subject in their studies.

Glossary sidebars define key words within the text.

At the end of the book, a summary Glossary lists the key terms defined in the volume. There is also a list of further print and Web-based resources and a full volume index.

About this book

This book covers all aspects of the Native American economy, from the growing or hunting of food to the manufacture and trade of goods and the development of early forms of currency, known as wampum. By the time Europeans arrived at the end of the 15th century, long-distance trade networks linked peoples all over the continent, and stretched south into what is now Central America. The book also describes the ingenuity with which peoples adapted to their environment, such as by learning to make paper from the bark of the birch tree or developing homes that could be easily dismantled and carried whenever the tribe moved to a new site.

The other major topic of the book is warfare, which among many native peoples was at least in part an economic activity. Groups raided neighboring tribes to seize captives to help farm or gather food, to seize stores such as corn, or to steal horses or livestock. As the book explains, warriors had a special status in many societies, and complex rituals and values surrounded their weapons and clothing.

From the 16th century onward, many native warriors found themselves fighting not among themselves but European or American settlers. This book describes most of the major conflicts that took place over some 300 years before Native American resistance finally came to an end. These conflicts are often termed "wars," although the numbers involved were usually relatively small by today's definitions, and the military action was often more like an ongoing series of skirmishes than a set battle. Nevertheless, these conflicts involved noncombatants on both sides and changed the shape of North American history.

Agriculture

The origins of agriculture in North America date back to between 10,000 and 12,000 years ago. It was the end of the last Ice Age, and global climate changes led to the disappearance of the larger mammals, such as mammoths.

Hunter–gatherers

People who obtain most of their food by hunting wild animals and eating plants gathered from the wild.

The earliest Native Americans, known as Paleo-Indians, were hunter–gatherers who depended on the larger mammals for food and survival. Because of the extinction of the large mammals, the Paleo-Indians had to rely more on fruits, seeds, berries, and roots for food and they started moving around seasonally according to the availability of plants. Each year, they would return to a site where they knew a specific food source would be available. Because plants were gathered regularly, only the stronger plants were able to grow. This led to the survival and harvest of larger, more nutritious plants.

Early agriculture

The Paleo-Indians were exploiting the natural growth of wild plants. Evidence of deliberate agriculture, including the cultivation of the soil and raising managed crops, dates from about 3600 BCE.

Hybrid corn

Corn deliberately created from two other types of corn.

Traces of hybrid corn have been found in Bat Cave, New Mexico. The Bat Cave hybrid corn is far more drought resistant than other types of corn. Yet the cobs of the hybrid corn are small, and there is no evidence that such domesticated plants were a major part of the people's diet.

People in the Southeast began to expand their agricultural base in about 1000 CE. New strains of corn allowed farmers of the Mississippian culture to grow hardier corn. They also grew beans, squash, and other local plants, such as sunflowers, in vast fields located outside their villages along the Mississippi River.

Warrior farmers

Since the Mississippians did not develop a system for watering their crops, they farmed on fertile river floodplains. As their population increased, they needed more crops, yet they could expand only by farming on floodplains used by neighboring tribes. This led to competition for territory. As a result, the Mississippian culture became aggressive and warlike.

Much of the work involved in cultivating crops was paid as tribute by members of defeated tribes. Tributes could range from forced work in the fields to annual payments in agricultural produce.

Lack of rainfall

Mississippian culture began to decline about 1300 CE, when severe droughts ruined many of their farming areas. Despite the efforts of the shamans to conjure rainfall, the fields dried out and valuable seed crops were lost over a series of failed harvests. Land became even more valuable than before.

The Mississippians—who had been spreading out into small villages—began to occupy fewer but larger fortified settlements. These settlements were often protected by tall wooden fences and moats. In the 16th century, however, these settlements fell victim to the Spanish and French colonizers, who also destroyed the last fully functioning Mississippian culture: the Natchez. The colonizers introduced large-scale cotton and tobacco plantations into the region. To work these plantations, the Europeans imported slaves from the West Indies and Africa.

Mississippian legacy

Small-scale farming and traces of Mississippian-style practices continued into the more recent past in some Native American areas. Iroquoian peoples of the eastern Woodland, the Plains village tribes (Hidatsa

Curriculum Context

Students should understand the reasons for the rise and decline of the Mississippian culture.

Shaman

A person with special powers to access the spirit world and an ability to use magic to heal the sick and control events.

Plantation

An estate or farm on which crops such as tobacco are cultivated.

and Mandan) along the Missouri River, and seminomadic tribes, including the Osage and Pawnee, living along the major rivers of the eastern Plains and prairies all practiced agriculture.

The Iroquois kept garden plots of corn, beans, squash, and tobacco outside their woodland villages. They cleared forest areas by using the slash-and-burn method. However, as they soon learned, soil fertility drops quickly using this method, and Iroquois villages had to be moved every 10 years or so once the clearings became unproductive.

Slash-and-burn

Cutting down trees and undergrowth to make clearings and then burning the wood to fertilize the soil.

Seasonal agriculture

The Plains village and the seminomadic peoples who had moved west from the woodlands developed lifestyles based on eating both buffalo and corn. The Plains village tribes obtained buffalo meat by trade. The seminomads planted their fields in spring and then abandoned their villages to spend the summer months in pursuit of buffalo herds, a period when they adopted the hide-covered tepees of the nomads. They returned to their permanent villages in late fall for the harvest.

A parallel development occurred in the other main agricultural area, New Mexico and Arizona. This is a desert region, yet the Anasazi, Hohokam, and Mogollon ancestors of the modern Pueblo and of the Pima and Papago were

A European engraving, published in 1619, of Secotan, an Algonquian village on the Pamlico River in Virginia, shows fields of different crops.

building irrigation ditches and cisterns over 2,000 years ago. Corn, beans, and squash formed their staple diet, but they also raised tobacco and cotton in the Mimbres Valley and along the Gila and Salt rivers. So successful were they that they were able to harvest two crops a year, in March and August. In March, the young plants were available for immediate consumption. In August, the mature plants could be dried and stored for consumption in winter.

Adapting to drought

The droughts of 1300 CE were felt across the whole continent and caused dramatic changes in the Southwest. Large Anasazi and Mogollon villages were abandoned, and the people moved into more secure multistory adobe apartments in the recesses of cliff faces with small garden plots on the tops of the plateaus. The Hohokam moved into sheltered locations along river courses on the desert-valley floor.

Cliff dwellings had been abandoned by 1500. When the Spanish arrived in the 16th century, many Pueblos had already relocated their villages to the tops of isolated mesas, or plateaus. Their fields were widely scattered around the bases of the mesas. Much of a villager's life was spent cultivating and protecting crops.

Managing Pueblo farms

Although agriculture is no longer the main industry among Native Americans in the Southwest, many Pueblo villages retain outlying farming communities and emphasize agriculture in their ceremonial and social life. For instance, Pueblo villages are divided into two moieties, each having responsibility for running the affairs of the village for six months of the year. Thus spring and summer, when crops reach maturity, may be controlled by the Squash moiety; whereas winter activities may be directed by the Turquoise clans, who have greater responsibility for trading activities.

Adobe

Heavy clay, sometimes mixed with straw and made into bricks to be used for building.

Moiety

One of the two groups into which many Native American tribes were divided. Each was often composed of related clans, and marriage to someone of the same moiety was usually forbidden.

Alcohol

Alcohol had a major effect on the lives of Native Americans. Even before European settlers began to rely on alcohol as a bartering tool with native peoples, it was used in tribal rituals in some agricultural areas in North America. However, when white settlers began to migrate and trade across the continent, the use of alcohol became more widespread and had a profound and often negative impact on most tribal communities.

Pre-Contact
Before Europeans arrived in the Americas.

In Pre-Contact times, alcohol was an integral part of religious rituals in the Southwest and Southeast; the Papago and Pima used a fermented drink in a ritual intended to bring rain. Among tribes using alcohol for nonreligious purposes, such as drinking cactus wine in the Southwest and persimmon wine in the Southeast, moderation was essential. Public drunkenness might be severely punished; the Natchez of the Mississippi Delta considered intoxication an offense punishable by death. Even the well-known *tiswin* (corn beer) of the Apache had a low alcoholic content.

The Papago of the Southwest made an alcoholic beverage from the saguaro cactus. It was drunk during ceremonies to encourage summer rains.

Alcohol, settlers, and fraud
White settlers, especially fur traders, introduced stronger forms of alcohol. "Indian whiskey" became a

major trade item. This was a blend of whiskey, water, sugar or molasses, and virtually any other ingredient individual traders chose to add—pepper, spices, even gunpowder were all used.

Both traders and U.S. government representatives considered it acceptable to use alcohol to defraud the peoples with whom they dealt. Fraud and deceit, fueled by alcohol, were commonly used to trick intoxicated chiefs to sign away lands in false treaties. For example, the Fort Wayne Treaty of 1809 resulted in millions of acres of Native American land being illegally "sold" to the governor of the Indiana Territory.

The actions of intoxicated individuals, both Native American and white, could lead to violence and unrest. Many skirmishes between Native Americans and white settlers were triggered by excessive alcohol.

Alcohol abuse and control

Although the U.S. authorities passed laws limiting or banning the trading of alcohol to Native Americans, their representatives often turned a blind eye to the activities of whiskey peddlers. In May 1873, the Canadian government authorized the formation of the Royal Canadian Mounted Police (Mounties) specifically to combat the illegal trade in alcohol.

In the United States, alcohol abuse is still a problem, particularly among young Native Americans who have been educated in white schools and find themselves alienated from their traditional way of life. Modern reservations often declare a no-alcohol policy, but it has failed to prevent independent traders setting up liquor stores just outside reservation boundaries. Active cooperation between tribal councils and government agencies, together with greater opportunities and an increased sense of Native American pride, are slowly reducing alcohol abuse.

Curriculum Context

Students might consider the extent to which alcoholism among Native Americans today is one of the legacies of 19th-century federal policies.

Birchbark

The bark of birch trees was very important to the peoples of the northern woodland. It was used extensively by Algonquian-speaking groups, which spread from New Brunswick to the Mississippi, and by Athapascan peoples of the lower Yukon. Similar use was made of heavier, more durable elm bark by the northern Iroquois and other peoples of the Great Lakes region.

Curriculum Context

Students can compare the use of birchbark in the northern Woodland with Northwest Coast people's reliance on cedar for their houses and artifacts.

Multifunctional material

Large sheets of bark could be peeled from either birch or elm trees. The Algonquian-speaking peoples of the Great Lakes and the Naskapi of Labrador sewed several sheets together to make long birchbark rolls. These could be placed over a framework of bent poles to make conical or tent-shaped lodges, or wigwams. The Sauk, Iroquois, and others covered large communal houses with whole sheets of elm bark.

Birchbark canoes

Perhaps the best-known use of birchbark was in making canoes. The Subarctic has many small streams, rocky points, and rapids over which canoes had to be carried. Strips of birchbark fixed over a framework of cedar splints made an effective and lightweight boat that could be easily carried over obstacles by two people. The joints between the bark sheets were sewn with pine roots and made watertight with pitch.

Subarctic

The region immediately south of the Arctic that includes much of Alaska and Canada.

Throughout the Subarctic, bark containers were common. For cooking food, the containers would be filled with water, then small stones that had been heated through would be dropped into the water, bringing it to boil. Bark containers were also used as buckets, bowls, trays, and cups. These were decorated with designs that were either engraved or made by scraping through the thin, brown inner layer of birch. Alternatively, the containers were painted in geometric

Thirteen species of birch trees grow in North America. They are especially numerous in damp woodlands and by streams and lakeshores.

and naturalistic patterns. Bark containers made by the Ojibway and Micmac have typical engraved and scraped styles of decoration, although the Micmac are better known for bark boxes intricately embroidered using porcupine quills.

Useful decorative objects

Winnowing trays for wild rice were made by the Ojibway. The Cree produced deep storage containers by folding and sewing strips of bark. Watertight pans of folded bark were used for collecting maple syrup by both the Ojibway and Penobscot. Among the Athapascan tribes of the western Subarctic watertight bowls were similarly made by folding and sewing bark.

The Ojibway and Athapascans also made cut-out shapes of bark purely for decoration, although these would occasionally be used as templates for beadwork or engraving. "Transparencies" of paper-thin strips of bark were also made for amusement. The bark was bitten to make intricate patterns that were clearly seen when held up to the light.

Canoes, patterns, and rituals

An unusual use of bark unique to the Ojibway and their allies in the Three Fires Confederacy was bark rolls that were elaborately engraved with symbols and used as a reminder by priests when conducting ceremonies of the Grand Medicine Lodge, or Midewiwin. The priests would "read" the symbols to determine seating arrangements or to remind themselves of the order of a complicated series of songs.

Three Fires Confederacy

A group of Algonquian-speaking peoples based around the Great Lakes.

Midewiwin

A medicine society whose members perform curing rituals, using healing herbs and mysticism to promote physical and spiritual well-being.

Bows and Arrows

The bow and arrow was one of the most important traditional Native American weapons. Unlike a rifle or a pistol, a bow made no noise or flash of igniting powder that could give away a warrior's position. Arrows could also be launched from a bow at a far higher rate than balls could be fired from a musket or early types of rifle.

Repeating firearms

Guns that load multiple cartridges when the trigger is set.

Sinews

The strong, cordlike tendons and ligaments that attach muscles to bone.

Watching Plains men hunting buffalo in the 1830s, the American painter George Catlin estimated that 15 to 20 arrows could be launched within a minute—only repeating firearms could match that rate of fire. Native Americans did not acquire quick-loading rifles and repeaters until after the 1860s, and even then, they continued to carry a bow and arrows as backup.

Native Americans crafted their bows out of wood or, more rarely, horn or bone. People would often travel for several hundred miles to obtain Osage orangewood for bow-making. This particularly strong, flexible wood was a major trading item between peoples. For extra strength and flexibility, they often covered bows with animal sinews. Sinew-backed bows had five times the power of standard ones. Sinews were also used as bowstrings.

Powerful and deadly

Power was a major feature of Native American bows. A well-made arrow shot from a strong bow at close range could go straight through a human skull, a horse, or even a buffalo.

U.S. Army medical reports from the mid-1800s tell of terrible wounds caused by arrows. One soldier died after being struck by three arrows, the point of one driving through his guts. Another man was hit by nine arrows, one sinking several inches into his buttocks.

Generally there were two types of arrow: hunting arrows and war arrows. Buffalo and deer move on four legs, so their ribs are vertical. Native Americans fashioned their hunting arrows so that their tips would fly through the air vertically, slipping easily between an animal's ribs to strike its vital organs. War arrows were designed to fly with their tips horizontal so that they passed easily between human ribs.

In this dance, photographed in 1908, Atsina men shoot arrows up into the sky.

More than just piercing

Even if a war arrow did not strike a vital organ, death was likely from poisoning or infection, since the tips of war arrows were often contaminated with snake venom or some kind of rotting animal matter. Unlike hunting arrows, war arrows also had barbed heads that could not be pulled from the victim's body without causing further damage. Special surgical tools were needed, or the arrow had to be pushed clear through the body or limb and out the other side. In addition, the arrowheads were only weakly attached to the shafts with glue that tended to melt from body heat. If a war arrow was not removed within about 30 minutes, the tip would work loose, and the two parts would have to be pulled out separately.

Buffalo

The buffalo, or bison, has been called the "staff of life" of the Great Plains peoples. It was central to their survival. The near extinction of this powerful animal paralleled exactly the decline of the peoples that roamed the Great Plains.

Ice Age
The most recent period of widespread glaciation, when ice sheets extended over much of the North American continent. It peaked around 20,000 years ago and ended around 8,000 years ago.

Ancient beast

It is now believed that people began hunting buffalo more than 15,000 years ago. Excavations in 1926 at a site in New Mexico near the Cimarron River uncovered spear points embedded in the carcasses of Ice Age bison (*Bison antiquus*). The find was remarkable in that it swept away the belief that humans entered the Americas a mere 3,500 to 4,500 years ago.

Bison antiquus was displaced by the spread south of the smaller *Bison occidentalis* about 12,000 years ago. *Bison occidentalis* was itself ousted in 6000 BCE by the arrival of the modern buffalo, *Bison bison*. Both Ice Age and modern bison were attracted to the Great Plains by the availability of nutritious grasses, and human hunters were attracted by the herds.

For early Native Americans, bison were a major factor in the development of cooperative hunting. They also increased the status of those who had outstanding hunting skill or who, by more mysterious means, had the power to draw the herds close to the camps where they could be hunted more easily. During tribal gatherings, hunting groups often killed several hundred buffalo by driving them over a cliff edge.

Tepee
A cone-shaped tent built with a pole framework and traditionally covered with animal skins.

The great provider

Buffalo provided human communities with almost all the necessities for survival: in addition to large quantities of meat, the hides could be used as covers for tepees or for thick and warm buffalo robes and bedding; bones provided tools; the hoofs could be boiled down into a strong glue; the thick neck skin was heat-shrunk for shields; the paunch served for carrying water; the tail could be turned into a fly whisk; and the sinews were adapted as ropes and cords. Even dried dung, known as buffalo chips, provided a slow-burning but intensely hot fuel for cooking.

To the Plains people, the buffalo was a remarkable, almost magical, creature. It is no surprise, therefore, that the buffalo occupied a major place in their myths and ceremonies. Its skull served as a sacred altar during the most important tribal rituals: those of the Annual Renewal Ceremonies, or Sun Dance.

Sun Dance
An important ceremony practiced by Plains peoples to celebrate the renewal of nature.

Calling the herds

Shamans (medicine men) with power believed to be derived from buffalo were held in high esteem and awe. The Beaver Men of the Blackfoot were believed to possess the power of summoning the buffalo when meat was scarce. Other peoples placed similar faith in their own practitioners. For example, the Cheyenne's Hoof-Rattle Society (a group of medicine men) owned a section of grooved elk antler carved in the form of a rattlesnake. When this was rubbed with an antelope shinbone and held against a piece of buffalo rawhide to amplify the sound, it emitted a shrill tone that the buffalo were said to be unable to resist. To call buffalo herds, the Pawnee relied on staffs made from spruce poles wrapped with red and blue streamers and decorated with beadwork and eagle feathers.

Forced extinction
The importance of the buffalo to Plains cultures helps explain the sudden and disastrous collapse of Native American resistance to the territorial advancement of white settlers. During the early 19th century, the Plains were still "Indian country," but by the mid-1800s numerous U.S. Army posts had been established in the region. These military posts employed hunters to supply the garrisons with fresh buffalo meat. Frequently, only choice cuts of meat were taken.

Garrison
A place where troops are stationed.

Curriculum Context

The buffalo is a good example to consider when comparing the ways Native Americans and Europeans exploited natural resources.

Buffalo were hunted almost to extinction in the 19th century. By the 1880s, only a few hundred remained but conservation efforts over the last century have increased that figure to around 350,000.

At the same time, professional buffalo hunters interested only in obtaining hides to be sold as fashion accessories, mostly on the East Coast, were decimating the great herds. The Plains grasslands became a graveyard of rotting and stinking buffalo carcasses. Noting the dependency that the Native Americans had on the buffalo, U.S. military officials realized that destroying herds in the vicinity of native villages was a certain—and relatively safe—method of forcing them into submission. Without buffalo, the people had to choose between starvation and surrender to the United States. By surrendering, they were at least able to receive food rations from the U.S. government.

Several Native American groups fought back in an attempt to save the buffalo, but it was an unequal battle. When railroad tracks were laid across North America after the 1860s, severing the migration routes and disrupting the vital breeding patterns of the buffalo herds, the destruction was nearly complete. Yet a few herds survived in remote areas, and today buffalo in North America are a protected species.

Canoes

The eastern woodlands, Arctic, Northwest Coast, and California all depended on water transportation—either along rivers and streams or on the open sea. The different needs in each area, as well as the availability of raw materials for boatbuilding, determined the type of craft Native Americans made.

Canoes for use in wooded and forested areas had to be easily maneuverable and light enough to carry across portages—areas of rivers blocked by rapids or where a cross-country journey had to be made from one river to another. Elm and birchbark strips were sewn together over a wooden framework and had joints sealed with pitch. This made a canoe that was fragile but ideally suited to its environment. It was light and could easily be patched and mended using readily available materials.

Inuit Kayaks

To the north, in the Arctic, wood and bark were scarce and seas were often rough and partially frozen. A fragile canoe would not have survived, and it was essential that a boat protected those inside from the harsh elements. The Inuit solved these problems by using any available material, such as driftwood or ivory, for the frames of skin-covered kayaks—small, one- or two-person canoes. These were covered with hides in which the only opening was a laced "hatchway" that fastened tightly around the paddler's waist. It stopped any water getting into the craft when it was being used on the turbulent Arctic Sea.

Heavy hunters

Along the Northwest Coast—from southern Alaska through British Columbia, and into northern California—the environment and social needs were different again. This is a rain-forest region, largely made

Pitch
A mixture of resin from a coniferous tree, animal fat, and charcoal.

Ivory
The material a mammal's tusk is made from, such as that of a walrus.

up of huge, straight-grained cedar trees. The people who lived in this region were more seafarers than river dwellers. They often hunted seal, walrus, and whale, as well as making long trading journeys by canoe through the treacherous waters off the coastal islands. They needed sturdy craft, with enough weight and balance, and so they made massive dugout canoes from solid cedar logs. Some of these craft were more than 50 feet (15 m) long, with elaborately decorated and carved prows and sterns. The decoration acted as a kind of branding to show to whom the canoe belonged.

Reed rafts

Farther south, in central and southern California, the climate was far milder. Although suitable timber for canoe building was scarce, there was plenty of tule reed. This could be tied into bundles and lashed together to form effective rafts, or balsas. Since tule absorbs water, and the rafts became waterlogged after a period of use, they would have been useless in areas that had a rainy climate. However, the climate in this region ensured year-round sunshine; when they were not in use, the balsas could be drawn up on beaches, where they quickly dried.

Specialized boats

Although bark canoes, kayaks, dugouts, and rafts were the major forms of river and sea craft, other forms of boat were used in more specialized areas. The Plains peoples of the Upper Missouri River, for example, made circular coraclelike "bullboats" covered with buffalo hide, which they used for river crossings. The Chumash of the Santa Barbara area in California made a unique canoe from split-wood planks lashed together and caulked (sealed) with asphalt.

Clothing

The popular image of Native Americans is of men dressed in fringed buckskin shirts and leggings, moccasins, and a flowing feather headdress. Native women typically wear long skin dresses with elaborate beadwork decoration. This image is all the more vivid because at many modern powwows Native American men, women, and children are all dressed in this way, regardless of their particular tribe.

However, such clothing was previously worn only by tribes of the central and northern Great Plains and, even within this limited area, it was worn only on special tribal or ceremonial occasions. More often, Plains men wore a loincloth and moccasins, while women wore plain dresses made of animal skin. In bad weather, men wore a loincloth together with leggings and a shirt. Both men and women used robes and blankets for extra warmth in cold weather.

Clothes and climate

Climate and available materials were the most important factors in Native American clothing. The early Paleo-Indians, who were hunter–gatherers and had to cope with extreme climates, were reliant on furs and skins. However, the development of agriculture in the Southwest and Southeast meant that animal skins were gradually replaced by wild plants and cultivated cotton, which became the principal clothing materials.

Even today, the traditional dress of the Pueblo is a woven cotton kilt for men and a manta, or coarse cotton dress, for women. Native Americans took inspiration from Spanish designs for the manta.

Up to the 18th century, Native Americans wore the most appropriate clothing for the local weather conditions. In warmer regions, men and women either

Moccasins
Shoes made of one piece of deerskin or soft leather, stitched together at the top.

Hunter–gatherers
People who obtain most of their food by hunting wild animals and eating plants gathered from the wild.

went naked or wore a loincloth (men) or a short apron (women). Timucua women in Florida, for example, wore only a short netted apron of moss, although their bodies were covered by extravagant tattoos. The warm Californian climate also encouraged people to wear a minimum of clothing, and women in that region wore aprons made of fiber and decorated with shells and seeds. After contact with Europeans, however, Native Americans became more concerned with being modest and covering their bodies.

Inuit and Aleut clothing

At the opposite extreme, the severe conditions of the Arctic and Subarctic meant that clothing had to be wind- and waterproof as well as warm, and the Inuit and Aleut used virtually everything they could find in the most ingenious ways. In parts of Inuit territory, caribou skins were commonly used for clothing—as they were by the Algonquian- and Athapascan-speakers who shared the northern Subarctic regions with the southernmost Inuit groups.

The Inuit also used furs from polar bears and wolves, sea mammal skins, the furs and skins of smaller mammals and birds, fish skins, and seal intestines to make specialized cold-weather clothing.

Inuit and Aleut clothing was designed with two purposes: to prevent the damp and wind chill from getting through, and to allow the use of insulating pockets of air. The first task was achieved with waterproof materials. Fish skins and seal intestines are light and fragile, but they are almost totally wind- and waterproof. These materials were used for parkas, mittens, and other outer garments that could be worn over clothing in wet and windy conditions.

Instead of relying on bulky furs to keep out the cold, the Inuit wore several layers of loose-fitting clothes.

Curriculum Context

Students can usefully compare the diversity of clothing among Native American peoples and relate it to the natural resources and climate of each region.

These layers of clothing trapped pockets of air but were fastened tightly at the wrists, ankles, and neck to prevent the damp from entering. Another way of keeping out water was to sew garments from the inside with stitches that did not go through the outside layers. In severe conditions, the pockets of air would be filled with down (soft, fluffy feathers) or moss to provide extra insulation for the wearer.

Farther south

The Native Americans of the Northwest Coast, who lived in a temperate (moderate) rain-forest area, used the shredded inner bark of the cedar tree to make rain capes and hats. For ceremonial occasions, they made blankets out of dog hair and mountain-goat wool, which bore the totemic emblems of a clan's ancestry. In woodland areas that had plentiful deer, clothing was

Clan

A social unit consisting of a number of households or families with a common ancestor.

A group of Chilkat men and boys poses in ceremonial dancing costumes in around 1895. The Chilkat are part of the Tlingit group, who live in Alaska.

made from deerskin. Peoples in barren areas with fewer large game animals, such as the Great Basin, made blankets and robes out of strips of rabbit fur.

Clothing today

In the 20th century, Native Americans have adopted practical work clothes, such as blue jeans, check shirts, and cowboy boots, which they buy at local stores.

However, clothing is often given "meaning" by the addition of Native American elements: baseball caps are decorated with beads, and Stetsons have feathers inserted in the hat band. Both men and women wear beaded necklaces, braided hair, and tribal jewelry to emphasize their native identity.

A young Quinault girl, photographed in around 1913, wears ornaments made from shells. The Quinault are an ethnic group of the Northwest Coast, living in Washington State.

Corn

Corn was as important to the native farmers of North America as buffalo were to the nomadic hunters of the Great Plains. Corn (also called Indian corn or maize) was the dominant Native American crop, providing farmers with more food than all other crops combined.

An important part of the diet, corn also provided stalks that could be woven into thatch and husks for twined baskets. The Woodland Iroquois peoples wove masks out of cornhusks, while the Plateau Nez Percé used husks for making soft, twined bags.

Corn in America

Indian corn belongs to the grass family and is of American origin. Christopher Columbus introduced it to Europe in 1492, and there is no archaeological, linguistic, or historical evidence that corn existed in Europe before then. However, in the Americas, cobs of corn from archaeological sites and burials, as well as other objects decorated with pictures of corn, imply that it existed 5,000 years ago in North America and even earlier in Mesoamerica (the area from central Mexico to Nicaragua).

First hybrids

No one has discovered a wild species of corn, and its origins remain fairly obscure. The closest relative of cultivated corn is a grass known as teosinte (from the Aztec word *teocintli*), which was used as a food plant in Mesoamerica. Crossed with pod corn (the earliest type, dating from 3500 BCE, was found at Bat Cave, New Mexico), teosinte produces fertile hybrids with the strength and vigor of teosinte but with the nutritional value of corn. Hybrids such as this enabled Indian corn to play an important role in the agricultural economies of the New World.

Curriculum Context

Tracing the rise of cultures such as those in Mesoamerica from hunter-gathering to farming is included in many curricula.

Bat Cave

A complex of rock shelters, which were occupied for about 10,000 years and contained corn kernels more than 3,000 years old.

The multicolored ears of an old variety of corn, typical of that grown by Native Americans in the past but unlike that we grow and eat today. Native peoples ground corn between stones to produce corn flour.

Different varieties

When Columbus first encountered them, Native American farmers were growing virtually every type of corn known to the modern world, including dent (the most commercially productive), early-maturing flint corn, flour corn, sweet corn, and even popcorn.

Varieties of corn were grown in the Americas from Canada to Chile, but the most important corn-growing centers in North America were the Southeast, among the Mississippian temple-mound builders, and the Southwest, among the ancestors of the Pueblo, Papago, and Pima.

Soil and water

The Mississippians in the Southeast relied on the rich alluvial floodplains along the Mississippi and its tributaries for the fertile soil in which to plant their

Mound builders

Native Americans who built earth mounds for burial and ceremonial purposes.

Corn farming

To plant corn, Native American farmers first built up a mound of earth and made a hole in the center with a digging stick. They then dropped four or five kernels of corn into it. Farmers planted corn in between beans and squash. The dense cover provided by the squash reduced the growth of weeds, so that corn patches could be left alone until the crop ripened. This was vital to seminomadic Plains farmers, who planted their crops and then left their villages for a time to go on long buffalo hunts. The corn stalks also provided support for the bean plants.

crops. The arid Southwest, however, could be made fertile only by irrigation and water storage and distribution. The Hohokam ancestors of the Papago and Pima built wide, shallow canals, often over 10.5 miles (17 km) long and controlled by dams with valves made of woven mat that redirected water to the fields.

Rituals and worship

Corn was so vital that its cultivation could not be left to chance and the farmers' skillful hands. Elaborate rituals and celebrations were created to secure the help of the gods, ensure that the Corn Spirits would act kindly, and give thanks for successful harvests.

The sacred stories of the Corn Mother retold the ancient myths of the Animal Masters. This was a time when people and animals lived in harmony and the people spoke a common language but diverted the source of fertility and new life into the corn plants.

The Green Corn ceremony of the Southeast was both a thanksgiving at which roasted ears of green corn were dedicated to the gods and a ritual to bring fertility and growth to the crops and the people.

Southwestern kachinas (who were represented by masked dancers) were rain-bringers—moisture was vital in these desert regions—and the guardians of fertility. Kachin Mana, the Kachina Mother, is still an important presence at kachina dances today, as are the three Corn Maidens: Sakwap Mana (Blue Corn Maiden), Ang-chin Mana (White Corn Maiden), and Takus Mana (Yellow Corn Maiden). The Corn Maidens, in turn, are helped by Masao Kachin-Mana, who brings rain, and also by the Corn Kachina.

Kachinas

Spirit beings in the religion of Pueblo cultures. Dolls representing kachinas are carved and given to children to educate them. In ceremonial dances, people dress as kachinas.

Counting Coup

In order to gain status, a Plains warrior needed to gain war honors, also called "coups." A number of acts were regarded as coups, such as taking an enemy's gun, stealing a tethered horse from an enemy camp, or even scalping an enemy. However, one of the most highly prized war honors was counting coup.

To count coup was to touch an enemy with the bare hand or with an item held in the hand, such as a special coup stick, without doing him any injury. The warrior himself then had to escape unharmed, and his act also needed to be witnessed for it to count. Counting coup demanded great bravery and made the victim appear to be a poor or lesser warrior.

The honor system

A warrior who had touched his enemies many times with the coup stick was regarded as very brave. One such warrior was the Crow's most famous chief, who was called Plenty Coups. The Crow actually preferred to count coup against their foes rather than to scalp. To the Assiniboine warriors, counting coup in battle was considered far more important than killing their enemy. In both the Crow and Assiniboine tribes, four people might count coup on the same foe during a battle, although the honor bestowed on each warrior lessened with each successive coup.

Plains peoples counted coup against each other and against whites. At the Battle of Little Bighorn in 1876, the Cheyenne warrior Yellow Nose counted coup against General Custer's troops with their own flag.

Today, the honor of a warrior is celebrated in the homecoming dances that mark the safe return of Native American enlisted men and officers.

Curriculum Context

Counting coup is one of the customs to consider when comparing Native American and European attitudes to warfare.

Feathers for Warriors

Feathers were a prominent feature of Native American warrior costume and weapons. In addition to decoration, they were believed to have supernatural properties that would help those carrying or wearing them.

Feathers had practical uses, too; eagle and wild turkey feathers attached to the back end of arrows made the arrows far more aerodynamic and accurate.

The power of the eagle

The feathers from birds of prey were highly prized by Native American warriors, who admired and respected the birds' power, aggression, and speed of attack. They used the feathers of birds of prey to decorate their shields, lances, tomahawks, and coup sticks. The white, black-tipped feathers of the young golden eagle were particularly valued. Plains warriors also used golden-eagle feathers to decorate their calumets (peace pipes).

Lance
A spear used by warriors on horseback.

Nowhere, though, were feathers more prominent than in warrior headdresses. Once again bird-of-prey feathers were favored. For example, Apache and Navajo warriors adorned their war caps with owl feathers, which were believed to help the wearer avoid danger. But there were other uses and meanings as well. One Sioux chief said that the feathers he wore in his hair stood for the enemies he had killed in battle.

Among the Plains tribes, war honors, or coups, were important to a man's status, and warriors wore eagle feathers in their hair so that their achievements could be recognized. A code of cuts and markings on feathers, and how a feather was worn, denoted the type of war honors a warrior had gained. The codes varied according to the tribe. A Dakota–Sioux warrior, for example, who had been wounded a number of times wore a feather split in two along its shaft. If a

Chief Joseph of the Nez Percé photographed wearing a war bonnet. He was the leader of his people from 1871 to 1904.

Hidatsa warrior had a feather in his hair decorated with a red horse-hair tassel, it meant he had been the first to kill an enemy in a battle.

Mystical powers of feathers

Plains warriors also cherished feathers as part of their personal medicine. This was because the guardian spirits often appeared in the form of a bird, and that bird possessed characteristics the spirit gave to the warrior. Thus a hawk was valued for its ability to attack suddenly or an owl for its skill in striking silently. The young warrior would wear or carry the feathers of his guardian spirit whenever he went to war. This provided him with a link between himself and his guardian and a means to call on its power.

Curriculum Context

Warfare was common to many Native American groups, but the ways in which they related it to their spiritual beliefs differed.

Hunter becomes hunted

Some Plains warriors wore long headdresses, known as war bonnets, which consisted of dozens of eagle plumes. The plumes represented the war honors gained by a warrior society or by a tribe. The men who wore war bonnets were the most skilled and courageous warriors, so they became marked men in battle. Counting coup (touching the enemy without wounding him) on or killing a high-ranking warrior would be classed as an important war honor.

Firearms

Firearms, or guns, played a major role in the lives of many Native Americans, especially after the mid-19th century. Before then bows and arrows, spears, tomahawks, and other hand-held weapons used by Native Americans were a good match for the slow-loading muskets used by Europeans.

Only the best marksman could hit an individual enemy or an animal he was hunting at much more than a 50-yard (46-m) range. And a warrior could shoot several arrows in the time it took to reload a gun.

In the early 19th century, more accurate rifles began to replace the older muskets. Guns were also made that could be fired faster than before, but true repeating weapons became available only from about the 1860s. Only then were guns truly superior to bows and arrows.

Musket

A heavy muzzle-loading shoulder gun used by foot soldiers.

Using guns presented Native Americans with problems. Guns needed ammunition that could only be obtained from white settlers or traders. Nor did Native Americans have the skills in metalwork or other aspects of gunmaking to repair damaged weapons.

Useful guns

Even so, once native peoples came into regular contact with white settlers, guns soon became their preferred weapons for hunting and for war. About 1 in 20 of the warriors of the Plains owned a gun in 1800, but by the 1860s, most warriors had one. The importance of guns is also shown in other ways—the Blackfoot word for a great exploit in war meant "a gun taken."

The great advantage of guns, even from the earliest days, was in their stopping power—only the most accurate arrow fired by a warrior on a galloping horse from no more than 4 or 5 feet (1.2 or 1.5 m) away could kill a buffalo. A gunshot could kill an animal or bring an enemy down in battle without being as precisely aimed. Many Plains warriors became highly skilled at reloading and shooting accurately from horseback.

Relying on firearms

Firearms created a dependency on alliances and trade, not only for the guns themselves but also for ammunition, without which the firearms were useless. This trade relationship was important from the very first Native American–European contacts, and was welcomed and encouraged by Native Americans.

Annuities

Sums of money payable at regular intervals.

It was also one of the factors involved in securing Native American agreements to treaties: a considerable part of treaty annuities was paid in the arms and ammunition on which many tribes had become dependent in order to ensure their own security.

A source of division

Many whites opposed guns and ammunition being traded with or given to Native Americans, saying that they would only be used against whites in wars. However, stopping guns and ammunition reaching Native Americans could sometimes provoke a war. For example, the cutting off of ammunition supplies by the British was a cause of Pontiac's War (1763–1764). Native Americans came to rely on guns for hunting so without them the whole tribe might even starve.

During the 18th and 19th centuries, as firearms became more readily available to Native Americans, the balance among opposing tribes changed. This resulted in the forced migration of some peoples. Because of firearms, the Iroquois came to dominate the Great Lakes region in the 18th century, and the Ojibway forced the Sioux out of their homeland. By the mid-19th century, the Sioux had moved to the Great Plains and controlled large parts of the region.

Fishing

Fish was a primary food source for most Native Americans. Only in the Basin and Plains regions and in barren areas of the Southwest did tribes place a greater emphasis on other food types, such as buffalo and small game. If a group lived near fresh or salt water, then fish was a staple part of its diet.

Fishing in North America can be traced back to the earliest cultures that existed 10,000 years ago, and archaeological sites from most areas have yielded ancient fishhooks or harpoon points.

Primary food source

In some areas, fishing was the main source of nourishment. On the Northwest Coast and in the Plateau regions, salmon was the staple diet, though trout and sturgeon were also major food sources. Salmon was so important that in native languages the word for "salmon" was often the same word for "fish" in general. Also, peoples living farther inland sometimes had no special name for the tribes who caught so much salmon; they simply called them "fish-eaters."

Salmon live much of their lives in the ocean, but at certain times of the year they return to the rivers where they were born to breed. When they do, they can be caught in huge numbers. Native Americans smoked and dried much of their catch. Dried salmon was a valuable trade commodity, sometimes being sent as far as 1,000 miles (1,600 km) from where it was caught to be exchanged for other goods.

These peoples also had many rituals and beliefs connected with salmon and salmon fishing. Some peoples of the Northwest, for example, always filleted their fish before they dried it or ate it and put the bones back in the river. This was a religious act, done

Curriculum Context

Students can explore the diversity in Native American societies by comparing the lifestyle of Northwest Coast salmon fishers with those of their whale-hunting neighbors.

as a sign of respect for the salmon spirit. It was believed that this ritual would ensure the return of salmon in large numbers.

Fishing and products of the seas and rivers were also important in other regions. Along the California coast, fish were caught and shellfish were gathered, fueling a trade between coastal and inland peoples exchanging marine products for mountain game.

In the eastern Woodland and Southeast areas, fish provided food to supplement a main diet of corn, beans, and squash. In Florida, fish were a much more important part of the diet. Florida peoples also used fish for jewelry—for example, many women wore brightly colored, inflated fish swim bladders as earrings.

Swim bladder
A gas-filled organ in a fish's body which controls its buoyancy.

Seal fishing
Seal fishing needed special boats. Seal canoes were streamlined and polished so that they glided quietly through the water—otherwise the seals would hear the hunters coming and escape. A seal boat was never dragged up the beach—it was carried carefully to make sure that the bottom did not become roughened. Oils from whales, seals, and other marine mammals were important trade items and were sent far inland.

Whales

The most exciting type of fishing was the whale hunting of the Northwest Coast peoples. The Nootka of Vancouver Island caught humpback and gray whales. There were important rituals to follow to make certain of a good catch and ensure the safe return of the whale catchers. The whalers would have to sneak up on the whale while it was swimming on the surface and harpoon it. The wounded whale would then dive for a time before surfacing again to be killed. It was dangerous work, because a whale could easily wreck one of the 30-foot (9-m) canoes used by the whalers.

Food

Food preparation and consumption were always a sacred activity for Native Americans, who believed that all life was linked together spiritually. They also believed that the plants and animals they lived on—such as buffalo, deer, fish, birds, plants, seeds, roots, and berries—allowed themselves to be captured and gathered, provided they were treated properly.

The incentive for the animal or plant was that being captured and treated in a respectful way ensured a return to the bosom of the Earth Mother, from where they would be reborn.

Fields were blessed before planting, and animal spirits were urged in prayers to sacrifice themselves for the people. This had been decreed in the distant mythical past, when the creative deities gave each thing a function and purpose. The function and purpose of humans were different, but not of a higher order, from those of everything else.

Food featured prominently in old legends and in ritual activities. In ceremonial dances, buffalo, deer, beans, turtles, eagles, and corn were represented, among other things. It was believed that the spirit of these things controlled people's survival, since without them people would starve.

Vegetables and grains

The range of food products used was extremely diverse. Among cultivated crops were corn—a staple food used for a variety of breads, cakes, puddings, and cereals—as well as squash, melons, gourds, pumpkins, beans, and chilies. Tomatoes and sweet potatoes were used farther south, in Mesoamerica. All of these were unknown in Europe before the arrival of Christopher Columbus and the Europeans who followed him.

Mesoamerica
The region and cultural area extending from central Mexico to Nicaragua.

Wild plant foods were put to equally varied uses. In the Great Lakes region, the staple was wild rice—actually a form of grass—and wild greens were used too, including dockweed, pigweed, purslane, goosefoot, marsh marigold, pokeweed, different ferns, milkweed, and dandelions. To these were added prairie turnips, wild onions, and a host of other roots and tubers, as well as many seeds and berries. In California, the acorn was a staple; acorn flour was used for bread as well as for thickening soups and stews.

A woman of the Pomo people of northern California uses a beater to shake seeds into her basket in this photograph from the 1920s. Traditionally, the Pomo were fishers, hunters, and gatherers.

Hunting and fishing

Hunting did, of course, play an important part in the original diet. Buffalo meat was essential to Plains cultures, but deer, antelope, and smaller game were also widely available. In the Woodland region, deer were most commonly hunted, but caribou and elk dominated farther north. In the Arctic and on the Northwest Coast, sea mammals and whales often replaced other hunted foods. Rabbits, opossums, squirrels, and various birds were also popular. In the Southwest, the wild turkey was domesticated as a food source, although other domesticated animals apart from dogs were absent. After cattle, sheep, and pigs were introduced by the Spanish, these too were adopted into Native American diets.

Coastal peoples hunted many different types of land animals, such as bear and mountain sheep, but they depended more on fish and animals from the sea and nearby rivers. Salmon were a staple on the Northwest Coast and in the Plateau region, but trout, sturgeon, carp, and catfish were also common. There were other sources of food too, such as shellfish, crayfish and lobsters, crabs, clams, oysters, and turtles, as well as seaweeds and kelp.

Curriculum Context

Curricula may expect students to investigate how different food resources lead to differences in lifestyles.

The importance of sharing

Every method of cooking was used to prepare and preserve food with the exception of frying. Roasting and broiling are still popular methods of preparing tender cuts of meat, but many Native American households usually have a pot of broth or soup constantly on the fire so unexpected visitors can be fed. Food sharing is, in fact, an essential aspect of Native American culture both past and present.

Breads and puddings are prepared in ovens. In the Southwest these are small beehive-shaped clay ovens, but elsewhere a large pit covered with leaves and hot ashes is used to prepare breads and cakes. The pit oven is also used for roasting meat, vegetables, and tubers.

Storing food

Foods taken in season could be preserved in different ways for later use. On the Great Plains, meat was cut into thin strips and sun dried as jerky or pulverized and mixed with mashed suet and berries to make pemmican (a concentrated dried food). Sausages made from a stomach lining filled with meat and herbs could be smoke dried, as could fresh fish. Fats and grease were melted down and stored in containers. In big-game areas, such as the Great Plains, buffalo and bear fat served as a kind of butter, whereas on the Northwest Coast the eulachon, or candlefish, was processed in vast quantities, formed a complement to many foods, and was a valuable trade item.

Fur Trade

The fur trade, which was controlled first by Europeans and later by Americans and Canadians, had an enormous impact on Native American life. Some peoples prospered, and all grew dependent on European goods. Others were virtually destroyed or forced to move hundreds of miles and adopt totally different lifestyles.

From the middle of the 16th century until the end of the 19th century, tribal and white relations were dominated by the fur trade. Many tribes exchanged furs for goods, such as metal traps, knives, guns, and beads. These items, and the trading for them, changed greatly the lifestyles and crafts of many peoples.

Earliest exchanges

In 1534, Jacques Cartier, a Frenchman, sailed along the St. Lawrence River. He made contact with Algonquian- and Iroquoian-speaking peoples and found a ready supply of animal furs. Many Native Americans were eager to trade the furs for European goods. By the 17th century, the French operated a trading empire that extended from the Great Lakes to the Hudson Bay.

Hudson's Bay Company

A trading company set up in 1670 in the Hudson Bay area of North America. It controlled the fur trade in the region for centuries, forming a network of trading posts and obtaining fur from local Native Americans in exchange for goods shipped from Britain.

The British established the Hudson's Bay Company to compete directly with the French. For decades, there were many conflicts between the French and the British, all involving the area's Native Americans.

Meanwhile, the Russians were exploiting the fur trade in Alaska and the Northwest Coast in a different way. The British and French relied on Native Americans to supply furs and so maintained friendly relations. The Russians forced local tribes to supply furs.

Enter the Americans

Throughout the 18th century, the major European powers explored vast areas and made trade

agreements with numerous different peoples. In the early 19th century, however, white Americans began to compete with Europeans. Rather than rely on Native Americans to bring their fur pelts into trading posts, American companies hired their own trappers and sent them into tribal territories, causing much hostility. Native Americans saw the trappers as trespassers and also understood that they would suffer a loss in trade goods by not supplying the furs themselves.

Ultimately, the fur trade undermined Native American traditions. Hunters became dependent on trading, while their wives were kept busy cleaning and tanning the hides. Some hunters became wealthy through trade and rose to positions of power and prominence unequaled in the pretrade period.

The end of the fur trade

In the mid- to late 19th century, the trade industry collapsed. There were two prime reasons for this: furs fell out of fashion in Europe and the animals most valued for furs were destroyed by overhunting. This had a devastating effect on tribes that depended on traders supplying them with goods and was one of the factors that forced many peoples onto reservations.

Bent's Old Fort National Historic Monument in Colorado is an adobe fur trading post, established in the 1840s and now a museum and visitor center. In the 19th century, traders, trappers, and Plains people traded here.

Reservation

An area of land set aside for a specific tribe, governed by a tribal council and with its own laws. Its contact with the federal government is through the Bureau of Indian Affairs.

Gathering

The earliest Native Americans (Paleo-Indians) were hunter–gatherers. Originally, their diet was a combination of large game that they hunted and plant foods that they gathered. However, toward the end of the Pleistocene era (10,000 years ago), climate changes led to the extinction of many large game animals.

The changes created new environments across North America. Both the loss of large game and the change in environments directly affected gathering. During this period, Paleo-Indians who lived in woodland areas, where there was lush vegetation, began gathering plants such as ferns. In drier conditions, such as the Southwest, Paleo-Indians relied on desert plants such as yucca and prickly pear. Along the coast, they began harvesting seafood. Many coastal archaeological sites have been discovered because there were shell middens found nearby.

Midden

A refuse heap.

Predominance of gathering

It is commonly believed that from 6000 BCE Native Americans were primarily nomadic hunters. They lived in small bands that roamed the land in search of game. They also ate vegetation. Until about 1000 BCE, the movements of the nomadic bands were erratic but later, bands returned to old campsites more regularly. These popular campsites were always set up close to rich sources of plant and vegetable materials. Several *manos* and *metates* (grinding stones and pestles) found at sites that date from this time indicate that these peoples relied on seeds, grains, and nuts.

Nomadic

Having no permanent home and moving from one place to another according to the seasons in search of hunting grounds, water, and grazing land.

The importance of plants and plant products may be underestimated for early Native Americans. This is because materials associated with hunting—such as bones and stone spear points—survive in the ground, but plant and material fibers decompose more rapidly.

Nootka women on the shores of Clayoquot Sound on Vancouver Island, Canada, photographed around 1910. They are gathering seaweed from the rocks and putting it in their baskets.

The case for gathering

Later cultures used plant products not only for food but also to make medicines and provide materials for clothing, footwear, and baskets. These uses may have been of greater importance than their use for food. Agriculture may have developed mainly to ensure a constant and reliable supply of raw materials, such as cotton and other fibers, for making everyday items.

There are other reasons to support the view that early Native Americans depended on gathered items. Evidence suggests that society was organized into small family bands. The band—a small cooperative of often related individuals—is ideally suited to using limited wild resources, whether of animals or plants. Tribal organizations, however, depended on communal hunting and farming to sustain the large numbers of people concentrated in one area.

Curriculum Context

Students should be able to explain why a gathering way of life leads to a social organization different from that in hunting or farming communities.

Traditional methods

Over the centuries, some Native Americans settled and became more dependent on agriculture. In most cases gathering was no longer necessary. However, other groups continued the practice of gathering in much the same way as their Paleo-Indian ancestors.

Horses

Discoveries at a number of archaeological sites have shown that early lithic hunters (big-game hunters who used stone-age technology) often killed horses for food. By the end of the last ice age (10,000 years ago), horses were extinct in North America. The last of the herds had migrated across the Bering Land Bridge into Asia and Europe.

The reason for this is uncertain, but scholars believe that the changing climate caused grasses to dry up, forcing the horses to look elsewhere for their fodder.

Reintroduced from Spain

There were no horses in North America from the time of their migration until they were reintroduced by Spanish expeditions in the early 16th century.

As Spanish forces moved north from Mexico into the Southwest region, they brought with them their means of transport—the horse. Trading horses to Native Americans was officially forbidden under Spanish law, but many horses ended up with the local peoples of the region nevertheless.

Ranches and raiding

The first Native Americans to come into direct contact with Spanish horses were the Pueblo of the Rio Grande, who tended herds at Spanish ranches. By the mid-17th century, nomadic groups that had moved into the Southwest and southern Plains areas, including the Apache, Kiowa, and Ute, had set a pattern of horse raiding that was to become typical of Plains cultures.

Pueblo Rebellion

In 1680, a dramatic event caused hundreds of horses to fall into Native American hands. This event was the Pueblo Rebellion—led by a priest of San Juan Pueblo

Curriculum Context

Some curricula ask students to explore how the introduction of horses changed intertribal relationships.

In this 1861 illustration, a Native American on horseback fires arrows into a buffalo to bring it down. By this time, Plains peoples had been using horses for around two hundred years.

called Popé—in which the Pueblo rose against their Spanish oppressors and drove them into Mexico.

Horsetraders and breeders

There was a fast spread of horses northward after 1680. Nomadic Southwest peoples bartered horses and products of the hunt to the seminomadic and farming peoples farther north. The Kiowa traded with the Wichita, Pawnee, Cheyenne, and Arapaho. The Ute traded with the Comanche and Shoshoni, while the Shoshoni traded with the Crow and Plateau tribes.

Soon the Nez Percé, Cayuse, and Palouse of the Plateau gained a reputation as horse breeders and traders, while the Mandan and Arikara villages on the Upper Missouri River became northern horse-trading centers.

Seminomadic

Usually moving around and living in portable or temporary housing but also having a base camp where crops are grown.

The increased mobility provided by horses attracted other groups into the area. Village and farming peoples of the river valleys became mounted hunters, and the Sioux and other peoples east of the Missouri acquired horses and moved onto the Great Plains, where they became nomads. By 1730, horses were owned by northern Plains peoples such as the Blackfoot, Assiniboine, Plains Cree, and Plains Ojibway.

A symbol of wealth

By the end of the 18th century, horses were widespread throughout the Great Plains. The buffalo, more easily hunted from horseback than on foot, became the basis of Plains Native American economies, and the horse itself became a symbol of wealth, honor, and prestige. A man without horses was "like a beggar" and dependent on others to loan him one if he was to be successful in communal buffalo hunts. Chiefs, whose reputation rested in large part on their generosity, often kept large horse herds in order to make such loans to the more needy members of the community.

Curriculum Context

Horses not only affected the ways Native American groups interacted but also had a huge impact on relationships and values within each group.

Eventually, horses became the basis of Plains social life. A young man hoping to marry was at a social disadvantage if he could not offer horses as gifts to his intended wife's parents. A man who wanted political power needed horses to prove he was worthy of an important position within the various warrior societies. The pressure to own horses was intense, and this encouraged horse raiding as a means of obtaining horses and as a way of demonstrating skill and bravery.

Hunter–Gatherers

Cultures based on both hunting and fishing or on gathering and farming were common in Native America. The combination favored in different regions depended on what resources were available and on what conditions—such as climate—existed.

Hunting and gathering is often thought of as a "halfway house" between early hunting and foraging groups and later, more developed, groups that grew their own food. However, in North America, adapting to the local environment was the deciding factor.

Early hunters

The earliest Native Americans (Paleo-Indians) were mainly nomadic hunters. Migrations into North America were prompted by the movements of large game animals, which small hunting bands followed. Initially, gathering was less important to these bands and was usually based on lucky finds rather than on planned searches. The inland areas to which they were drawn featured a wide variety of game animals, and the bands quickly organized into cooperative units during seasonal hunts.

Plants and climate change

The gradual warming of the continent at the close of the Pleistocene 10,000 years ago resulted in the extinction of many of the larger game animals. It also helped create several types of environments across North America, many of which supported a variety of plant foods in addition to small game.

Hunting–gathering communities grew quickly in a number of these vegetation-rich areas, such as the Northwest Coast and the Woodland region in the east. For thousands of years, the gathering of wild plant foods remained a major supplement to the diets of these peoples, even among those who developed

Curriculum Context

Many curricula ask students to trace the spread of human societies in North America, and food resources and climate play a significant role in this.

Pleistocene

The geologic time period between 1.8 million years ago, when the first humans appeared, and 10,000 years ago.

Curriculum Context

Comparing different hunter-gatherer societies is a useful exercise in appreciating the diversity of economic organization in Native American life.

farming. However, in some areas, hunting–gathering became the single most important economic consideration. Because of the organization needed for effective hunting and gathering, groups in California, on the Northwest Coast, and around the Great Lakes all developed very efficient societies.

The Californians

In the Pre-Contact period (before Native Americans first encountered Europeans), the area of present-day California was the most densely populated in North America. Groups with different languages and cultures were attracted here by the mild climate and abundance of resources.

Acorn meal

A coarse powder made from ground acorns.

The staple item gathered throughout much of California was acorn. Acorn meal was made into a variety of breads and cakes. It fed small coastal communities among whom hunting and gathering were equally important. These people also traded their gathered items for hides and meat acquired by tribes living in more mountainous areas.

The culture of these Californian people was very complex and skilled. They excelled in basketry—again using locally gathered plant materials—but were also famed for their skills in featherwork and for their development of complex political and social systems.

Great Lakes and wild rice

Conditions were rather different around the Great Lakes. Too far north to practice effective farming because of the short growing season, tribes here were dependent on another gathered item, wild rice. This grass grew freely in shallow waters around the perimeters of the lakes and was gathered by being beaten into mats held between two canoes.

Hunting

In prehistoric times, Native Americans were heavily dependent on hunting. Some, such as the Great Plains tribes, relied almost exclusively on the hunt, which provided meat, as well as hides and furs for clothing, bedding, and shelter.

Prehistoric hunters

Around 10,000 years ago, the first Native Americans hunted using spears and atlatls. They used these simple weapons to kill the massive game that roamed the land at that time, including woolly mammoths, mastodons, saber-toothed tigers, American lions, and bighorn bison. These larger game animals were beginning to die out because of the gradual warming of the continent. The early hunters also stalked giant beavers, armadillos, sloths, and tapirs and developed new hunting techniques, including miring animals in bogs, using fire to drive stampeding herds over cliffs, and capturing animals in a variety of traps and snares. These techniques were used to capture abundant game such as bison, deer, moose, elk, and caribou.

Originally, early Native Americans lived in small bands that roamed the land in search of food. Over the centuries, these bands formed alliances that eventually led to the creation of large tribes. Bands continued to spend most of the year on their own but came together seasonally for tribal hunts. Even then, individuals would hunt and trap alone, sharing the catch with the whole group or tribe.

Regional differences

In British Columbia and southern Alaska, salmon was the main food. However, hunters also stalked other animals, including bear and mountain goat. In the colder regions of Subarctic Canada, game varied according to the seasons. Among the larger animals hunted for both meat and hides were caribou, moose,

Atlatl

A spear thrower consisting of a rod or board with a hook or thong at the back to hold the spear.

This 1590 European engraving shows how Native Americans in Virginia killed alligators. The men are ramming poles down the animal's throat, turning it on its back, beating it with clubs, and shooting it with arrows.

musk oxen, deer, and wood-buffalo. Smaller game was trapped, including beaver, mink, porcupine, hare, and otter. Fishing and hunting of birds were also common.

Farther north, the Inuit and Aleut hunted caribou in southerly areas, but sea and ice mammals, such as seals and walruses, were their main prey. The Inuit also had specialized boats—called *umiaks*—to hunt whales. The Inuit and Aleut were also able to hunt polar bears, arctic wolves, arctic foxes, and arctic hares.

Hunting along the eastern seaboard depended on animals such as deer, small game, and birds. The peoples in the Everglades also hunted alligators.

Buffalo, horses, and guns

On the grasslands of the Plains, buffalo was the major game animal. Hunting was done by small groups on foot. In the 1600s, Plains groups began obtaining horses from the Spanish and started to acquire guns supplied by the English and French. From then on, the favored method of hunting buffalo was on horseback using a gun. Other techniques, such as drives over cliffs or surrounding a herd so it milled in confusion, were also used. Plains hunters also stalked deer, small game, antelope, and mountain sheep in mountainous areas.

Indian Wars

The Indian Wars were the last Native American resistance to white expansion. Also known as the Wars for the West or the Plains Wars, they began in the 1850s, long after most Native Americans had been forced onto reservations. They ended by 1890.

Distrust between Plains groups and whites had begun earlier. The Indian Removal Act forced groups beyond the "permanent Indian frontier" in the 1830s. In 1835, Texas declared itself independent from Mexico and then deliberately tried to exterminate the southern Plains peoples. At the same time, the Oregon and Santa Fe trails were established as wagon-train routes across the Plains. The scene was set for a tragic confrontation.

The beginning of conflict

In 1854, Sioux men found a wandering cow and killed it for food. A settler claimed the cow had been his and demanded compensation. The Sioux made an offer that was refused. A U.S. Army lieutenant called John Grattan, fresh from the military academy, took matters into his own hands and marched a detachment of troops into the Sioux village to make demands.

When the Sioux refused to give up the "thief," Grattan responded with artillery fire, killing a prominent chief. Within moments, his entire command was dead, riddled by Sioux arrows. The white public demanded revenge. In 1855, 1,300 troops destroyed a Sioux village on the Platte River.

In the following year, a petty argument about who owned a stray horse led U.S. troops to murder a Cheyenne family. The Cheyenne retaliated by killing a trapper. Troops then attacked and destroyed a Cheyenne village; the Cheyenne responded by plundering and burning two settler wagon trains. When 300 of the bravest Cheyenne warriors were

Indian Removal Act

A federal law signed by President Andrew Jackson in 1830 to authorize the removal of Native Americans from their lands in the east and their resettlement in the west.

Artillery

Heavy weaponry, such as cannons and rockets.

Saber

A sword with a curved blade and a hand guard, used by cavalrymen.

Curriculum Context

Students can compare 19th-century attitudes and policies of the U.S. government, army, and European settlers toward Native Americans.

Truce

A suspension of fighting by agreement of opposing sides.

routed by a saber charge at the Battle of Solomon Fork in 1857, peace came temporarily to the Plains.

Peace lasted only a short time. Gold was discovered at Pike's Peak in 1859, bringing 80,000 prospectors to the Plains over the next three years. The Native Americans thought these white men who dug in the dirt were crazy and left the prospectors to fight among themselves. But following them came lumbermen, traders, real-estate agents, and settlers.

Troops were brought in to protect the new towns, and volunteer militia forces were formed against "the Indian Threat." The most notorious of these was the Colorado Volunteers. Led by a former Methodist minister called J. M. Chivington, the Colorado Volunteers attacked a Cheyenne village on the false report that villagers had stolen cattle. The Cheyenne retaliated by killing innocent settlers but then agreed to a truce and set up their camps under army protection. Chivington led his Volunteers in a surprise raid, against army orders, on a village on the banks of Sand Creek led by Chief Black Kettle. The Volunteers massacred 200 Cheyenne women and children and later displayed their scalps and severed limbs in a Denver theater.

Open warfare

For the next three years, the Cheyenne fought bitterly, stopping only in 1868, when their war leader, Roman Nose, was killed. Roman Nose broke a personal war-protection taboo against eating meat with a metal object, and he knew he would die in the battle. History records this as the Battle of Beecher Island after an army lieutenant who died there. The Cheyenne remember it as "The Day Roman Nose Died."

Warfare now flared across the Plains. Between 1866 and 1890, the U.S. Army fought over 1,000 battles with Native Americans, sometimes burning villages and slaughtering their inhabitants. These were almost always friendly villages that were close to Army forts and presented easy targets. The general policy among whites was that "the only good Indian is a dead Indian."

Gold rush

Gold was discovered in 1866 in Montana. When the Sioux refused to give up the lands where the gold was, a protective string of forts was built along the Bozeman Trail. The Sioux, Cheyenne, and Arapaho, under the leadership of Red Cloud, besieged the forts.

A young lieutenant named William Fetterman, who boasted he could conquer all the Sioux with 80 seasoned troopers, was led into an ambush where his entire force was destroyed. He had 81 troopers with him. White America remembers this disaster as the Fetterman Massacre.

The forts were abandoned after 1868, after the Medicine Lodge and Fort Laramie treaties were signed. Under these treaties, the Powder River country and the sacred Black Hills were granted to the Sioux forever.

Despite the guarantees of the treaties, another force was sent to fight against the Cheyenne. Once again it was Black Kettle's innocent village that was attacked. Black Kettle was killed, but the army troopers were driven off by the arrival of Arapaho, Kiowa, and Comanche reinforcements. The officer in charge, in his first engagement with Plains Indians, was Lieutenant Colonel George Custer. In his hasty retreat he abandoned 19 troopers who had been sent into the camp to round up the village's horse herd.

Then, in 1874, gold was discovered in the Black Hills. An army detachment was sent to order prospectors off these sacred Native American lands, but the officer in charge, Custer, simply told the miners they were

Bozeman Trail

Named for John Bozeman, the Bozeman Trail connected the Oregon Trail with the goldfields of Montana, cutting across Native American lands.

Medicine Lodge Treaty

A set of three separate treaties signed in 1867 at Medicine Lodge Creek, Kansas, between the U.S federal government and the Kiowa, Comanche, Plains Apache, Southern Cheyenne, and Arapaho peoples. The treaties involved the surrender of tribal homelands in exchange for reservations in the Indian Territory.

Fort Laramie Treaty

A treaty signed in 1868 at Fort Laramie, Wyoming, between the United States and the Sioux and Arapaho peoples.

trespassing and reported that the gold fields were even more extensive than had been realized. The white settlers abandoned the 1868 treaty, and the Sioux under Crazy Horse and Sitting Bull fought back.

The last battles

The Sioux resistance led to some of the most spectacular clashes and campaigns of the Indian Wars. In 1876, General George A. Crook and 1,000 troops were defeated at the Battle of the Rosebud and forced to withdraw. Afterward the Sioux, with Cheyenne and Arapaho allies, set up camp on the Little Bighorn. Here, Custer and the Seventh Cavalry attacked them but were surrounded and defeated at the famous battle of the Little Bighorn.

The U.S. citizens, who in 1876 were celebrating their first centennial, were outraged. Numerous battles and skirmishes were fought until 1881, when the tribes were finally defeated. During this period, Crazy Horse surrendered and was murdered. Sitting Bull fled to Canada, returning to Dakota to surrender in 1881.

Finally, in 1890, the Indian Wars came to a tragic end. Some Sioux under the leadership of Big Foot attempted to join the now law-abiding Red Cloud. They were met at Wounded Knee by 500 soldiers of the reformed Seventh Cavalry, Custer's old regiment, armed with guns capable of firing explosive shells.

A shot was accidentally fired, no one knows by which side, and the cavalry opened a barrage of fire from their guns. Within 30 minutes, nearly 300 Sioux men, women, and children lay dead. It was three days after Christmas, and the Sioux were buried in a mass grave in front of a church bearing the Christmas greeting "Good Will to All Men."

Skirmishes
Frequent small incidents of fighting, often as part of a larger conflict or war.

King George's War

The term "King George's War" describes North American conflicts that took place during the reign of King George II of Britain (1727–1760). Like previous wars involving the Spanish, French, and British colonies in North America, it was part of a European conflict, in this case the War of Jenkins' Ear. This began in 1739 and became part of the larger War of the Austrian Succession fought in Europe between 1740 and 1748.

In North America, there were effectively two phases of fighting during King George's War, first in Florida between 1740 and 1742 and then in New England and Canada between 1745 and 1748.

Colonial rivalry

Since the end of Queen Anne's War in 1713, both the British and the French had continued their European rivalry by attempting to expand their influence in North America. The French had built up their colony in Louisiana and had begun trading north from there up the Mississippi. They had also developed their trade routes from Canada into the Ohio area and farther west into the Plains. To do so, the French developed new alliances with Native American peoples, helping the Ojibway in a conflict with the Fox in what is now Wisconsin, and joining the Creek and Choctaw in attacks on the Natchez, Chickasaw, and Cherokee in the Carolinas and lower Mississippi area.

The British fought back by consolidating their hold in the east. They strengthened their alliance with the Iroquois, who were enemies of the French-supported Algonquian tribal group.

Various British and French colonies also continued to take land from other tribes. The Delaware of Pennsylvania were swindled out of a huge area in 1735,

New England

The region of the United States first settled by the English from 1620. It includes Maine, New Hampshire, Vermont, Massachusetts, Rhode Island, and Connecticut.

Curriculum Context

Many curricula ask students to analyze the political relationship between French and Native American peoples in areas the French colonized.

and the Catawba in South Carolina also gave up much land in return for help from the colonists.

War in Florida

James Oglethorpe, a leading founder of the recently established colony of Georgia, led an invasion of Spanish Florida in January 1740. The main Spanish town of Saint Augustine was besieged but not captured. The Georgian colonists, however, successfully repelled an attempted Spanish invasion of the colony in 1742. After that, neither side had any clear military advantage over the other.

Raids and skirmishes

Only one large battle took place in the course of the war. In 1745, a force of 4,000 New Englanders captured the French fortress at Louisbourg in Nova Scotia.

Most of the fighting was on a much smaller scale. Raiding parties on both sides often consisted of a mix of colonists and Native Americans. The Mohawk people were the closest allies of the British, and the Abenaki people fought most often alongside the French.

Frontier settlements on both sides were regularly attacked, usually by small forces. There were many raids throughout the war in the Connecticut Valley area of New Hampshire in particular.

A combined French and Native American force also captured and burned Fort Saratoga, New York, in November 1745. William Johnson, a New York landowner, persuaded the Mohawks to join a British attack on the French Fort Saint Frédéric near Lake Champlain in 1747. The attack failed.

By 1748, neither France nor Britain had made any real gains. They continued to try to expand their territory, however, and were soon at war again.

King Philip's War

Between 1675 and 1676, the Wampanoag and some of their neighboring tribes, including the Narragansett and Nipmuck, mounted a series of attacks on the English colonies in Plymouth, Massachusetts, Connecticut, and Rhode Island. The raids were led by a Wampanoag sachem, or chief, named Metacom, whom the settlers called "King Philip." The conflict has, therefore, become known as "King Philip's War."

When Metacom took over the leadership in 1662, he sought peace with the English but also tried to form an alliance with the Algonquian against the English.

Growth of the colonies

There were about 125,000 Native Americans living in the region in 1600, but by the 1670s there were fewer than 20,000. Most of these deaths had been caused by diseases, inadvertently introduced from Europe, to which Native Americans had no resistance.

The English colonists cleared forests to make space for their crops and farm animals, depleting the resources of game and plants used by native peoples. Native Americans traded game with the colonists in return for European goods, but as game grew scarcer, the hunters were unable to pay for goods they had received. Instead, they were forced to sell land to the English.

The English were also anxious to convert native people to Christianity. Native Americans who adopted the Christian religion were forced to make their homes in so-called "praying towns" and to live in a completely European way, cutting off their family ties.

The conflict begins

King Philip's War began in June 1675, when Wampanoag warriors raided the town of Swansea.

Alliance
A group of nations bound together by an agreement.

Praying towns
Towns developed by the New England settlers in the 17th century for Native Americans to live in so that they would convert to Christianity and give up their traditional way of life.

Metacom created alliances with the Narragansett and Nipmuck, many of whom also joined in the attacks. Some Christian Native Americans and later the Mohawk chose instead to fight on the English side. The native people were as well-armed as the colonists and were far more skilled in moving through the forests and swamps and in living off the country.

Both sides suffered badly in the fighting, but the whites gradually gained the upper hand. Metacom was trapped and killed in August 1676.

The price of war

The war was disastrous for both white settlers and Native Americans. The colonists had about 90 small towns and 30,000 people in New England at the start of the conflict. Twelve towns were completely destroyed, and at least 600 colonists killed in the fighting. Another 40 towns were raided and damaged.

About 3,000 Native Americans were either killed in battle or starved because their food supplies were destroyed. Hundreds more were put into slavery. The Native Americans of New England could do nothing more to limit white expansion.

As the map shows, King Philip's War ranged over a wide area, almost 1,000 square miles (2,600 sq. km). In spite of the many raids that the tribes mounted, the English settlers slowly gained the upper hand.

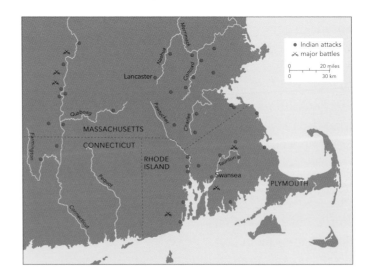

King William's War

King William's War is named after King William III of England, who was crowned in 1689. The fighting that took place in North America was part of a European conflict known as the War of the League of Augsburg, or the War of the Grand Alliance.

Britain and Spain were among the countries allied on one side, while France was on the other. The French and English colonies in North America and the Native Americans also became involved in the hostilities.

In North America, the Iroquois allied mainly with the British, while the French and the Abenaki tribe of what is now Maine were their most important opponents.

However, most of the other native peoples as far inland as the Great Lakes also fought against the Iroquois. This was partly the result of the long series of Beaver Wars that had been fought for much of the previous 50 years by the Iroquois League of Nations of northeastern peoples against many different enemies.

Hostilities begin

Fighting in the Maine area began in 1688, but the first major incident of the war occurred when a strong Iroquois army attacked the settlement of Lachine near Montreal in July 1689. About 200 French people and native allies were either killed or captured. The Comte de Frontenac, governor of the colony of New France (as eastern Canada was then called), had hoped to mount a full-scale invasion of New York but decided instead to adopt a quite different strategy.

De Frontenac called the new plan *la petite guerre* ("the little war"). There would be no big armies or large battles but instead many small raids to create destruction and an atmosphere of terror among France's British and native enemies.

Beaver Wars

Mid-17th century wars in eastern North America between the nations of the Iroquois federation and peoples of the Great Lakes region. The Iroquois tried, successfully, to expand their territory and control trade with Europeans in the region. In doing so, they pushed eastern peoples west of the Mississippi River and destroyed large tribal confederacies.

New France

The area of North America colonized by France up to 1763. This territory was eventually divided into five colonies: Canada, Acadia, Hudson Bay, Newfoundland, and Louisiana.

King William III of Britain, for whom the war was named, was a Dutchman of the Protestant faith. He was king only from 1689 to 1702.

Curriculum Context

Students should examine the legacy of King William's War on the Native groups of northeastern North America who took part in the conflict.

For their part, the British colonies mounted one major expedition against the French, in 1690, with a land and sea attack on Quebec. The French reinforced the town and the British attack failed. From then on, the British were limited mainly to defending their settlements against French and Native American raids.

Places such as Deerfield, Massachusetts, and Salmon Falls, New Hampshire, were among those heavily attacked at various times.

King William's War was fought with great brutality on each side, setting a pattern for the series of wars that was to follow through the next century.

Iroquois losses

The Iroquois did most of the fighting against the French. By the time the war officially ended in 1697, about one quarter of the Iroquois warriors had been killed, and the majority of their villages had been destroyed. About one-fifth of the 9,000 Iroquois died, more than the total of French and British casualties put together. Fighting actually went on until 1699, when the Iroquois were defeated in a battle with the Ojibway near Lake Erie.

Little Bighorn

In 1868, the U.S. government promised the Sioux in the Fort Laramie Treaty that the territory of the Black Hills (in present-day South Dakota) and other lands would remain the tribe's forever and that white people would be forbidden to enter. The peace and the treaty lasted for about five years with some minor violations. In 1874, the United States began to break the terms of the treaty in earnest when gold attracted prospectors to the area.

Breaking the treaty

The United States complained that some Sioux who had gone to live on reservations had not stayed there. They used this as an excuse to send an expedition led by Lieutenant Colonel George Custer to the Black Hills. Custer was supposed to be ensuring that the prospectors were not trespassing. In reality, his job was to discover whether gold could be mined in the area. He reported that there was plenty of gold, and prospectors began flocking in. The U.S. Army should have kept the gold miners out, but instead, the government decided to buy the land from the Sioux.

Prospector
Someone who explores an area for mineral deposits.

However, the Black Hills were regarded as sacred by the Sioux, and they asked a far higher price than the United States was willing to pay. The most important leaders on the Native American side were Sitting Bull of the Hunkpapa and Crazy Horse of the Oglala. Negotiations broke down in late 1875, and the United States announced that any Native Americans found outside the reservation after January 1876 would be hunted down as enemies. Extremely bitter winter weather made it impossible for the Sioux to travel to the reservations.

U.S. Army attacks

One U.S. Army force tried to attack an Oglala and Cheyenne village in the Powder River area in March

1876 but was driven back in freezing conditions and heavy snow. Large-scale fighting did not begin again until June. By then, Sitting Bull felt his men would defeat the U.S. Army. He had taken part in a Sun Dance and seen a vision of many soldiers falling in the Native American camp.

Three U.S. Army forces began moving toward the Yellowstone area, where many of the Sioux had now gone. The first of these, over 1,000 men under General George Crook, was forced to turn back after a tough engagement in the Battle of the Rosebud on June 17. Crazy Horse led the 1,200 or so Sioux warriors who fought in the battle.

Column

A long row of soldiers.

The overall U.S. commander, General Alfred Terry, still planned to close in on the main group of the Sioux with his other two columns. One of these, the 600 men of the Seventh Cavalry, was led by Colonel Custer.

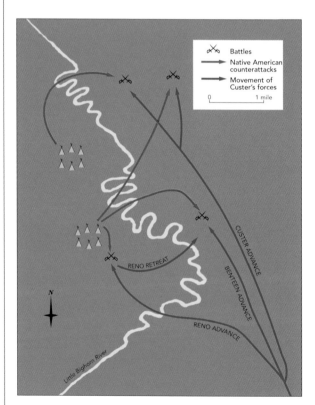

Custer's command

Custer's assignment was to attack the Sioux warriors in their camp and drive them toward the other U.S. Army group. However, he ignored what he knew from scouts was his enemies' strength.

Under Custer, Captain Frederick Benteen and Major Marcus Reno each had command of a group. Reno attacked first and retreated. Benteen then joined him, and the two forces combined and fought on. The Sioux who defeated Reno joined the attack on Custer's group.

Lieutenant Colonel George Armstrong Custer (1839–1876) was an experienced army officer when he took on the Sioux in 1876. After his death, he became a hero for white Americans.

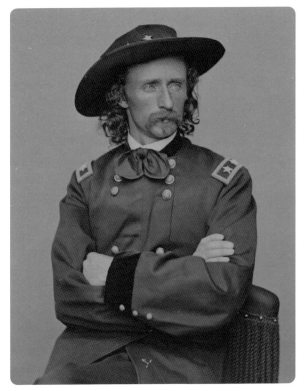

Early on June 25, Custer's scouts located the Sioux village near the Little Bighorn River, in what is now southeastern Montana, and he led his men toward it. Before attacking the village, Custer split his command into three groups because he was worried that the Sioux might escape, and he wanted to contain them.

In fact, it was Custer who was moving into a trap. The Native American village was huge, with people from every branch of the Sioux nation along with many Cheyenne and Arapaho. Custer and his 600 men were probably outnumbered about 10 to 1.

Custer's own section of the force, some 215 men, rashly moved in to attack and were almost immediately surrounded by Crazy Horse and his warriors. Within an hour, Custer and every one of his soldiers had been killed. The other two sections of the Seventh Cavalry were also fiercely attacked that day and the next, but managed to hold out in a desperate rearguard action.

The U.S. government and people in the East were shocked when the news reached them on July 4, which in 1876 also marked the celebrations of the U.S. Centennial. The army was immediately reinforced.

The Sioux seek peace

There were only two other large battles in the war. On November 25, the Fourth Cavalry successfully attacked a Cheyenne village in the Powder River area. In the Battle of Wolf Mountain in January 1877, Crazy Horse attacked an army camp but was driven off.

Afterward, an increasing number of Sioux leaders began deciding to make peace. They realized that they could not win in the end and that they could expect no mercy if they fought on after what had happened to Custer. Crazy Horse surrendered at Fort Robinson in May 1877, but was unhappy on the reservation. By September, General Crook was worried that Crazy Horse was encouraging other Sioux to go to war again and sent soldiers to arrest him. In the course of the arrest, Crazy Horse was stabbed to death.

Sitting Bull

Sitting Bull led about 4,000 of his people into Canada for a time. They had little food, and by the end of 1877 many had returned to the United States to live on the hated reservations. Sitting Bull himself did not return and surrender until 1881, by which time the few other bands of Sioux who had fought on had also been hunted down and killed or forced to give up.

Curriculum Context

Students can compare the strategies of Crazy Horse, Sitting Bull, and the chiefs who decided to continue fighting through 1877 and analyze the outcomes for all these groups.

White opinion

The following quote from an editorial in a New York newspaper sums up the general white opinion at the time: "It is inconsistent with our civilization and with common sense to allow the Indian to roam over a country as fine as that around the Black Hills, preventing its development in order that he may shoot game and scalp his neighbors. That can never be." The refusal to think of Native Americans as equals evident in the editorial and the complete dismissal of their rights emphasize how wide the barrier was between Native Americans and the whites.

Medicine

Traditional Native American medicine embraces a variety of activities besides dispensing potions for sickness and applying treatments for injury. These activities include clairvoyance, prophecy, divination, and states of ecstatic trance undergone by shamans (medicine men and women).

Native Americans believed that plants, animals, rocks, and all natural phenomena possessed "power"—the ability to reason and to motivate or influence objects and events. It followed, therefore, that disease had one of three causes: human, natural, or supernatural.

Cause and effect

Anything with an obvious human or natural cause—such as a broken bone or a flesh wound—was treated with natural herbs and concoctions. Many of these remedies proved highly successful, and more than 200 natural Native American drugs have appeared in the *Pharmacopoeia of the United States* since the publication of its first edition in 1820.

However, any sickness, disease, lethargy, or other ailment with no obvious human or natural cause was attributed to a mysterious, supernatural source.

Medicine and mystery

Medicine nearly always involved mystery. A shaman's power was mysterious because it came from the realm of the spirits and the supernatural. Cures were made through the intervention of the mysterious spirit sources with which a shaman was in contact. A shaman used ritual formulas, equipment, language, and chants to make contact with the spirits.

Ritual played an essential role in all aspects of Native American life, including war, art, and finding food.

Pharmacopoeia

A book describing drugs and medicines and how to prepare them.

Curriculum Context

Medicine and health are subjects which students can explore to compare Native American and European ideas, values, and religious beliefs.

Ritual and medicine, or mystery, were linked with everyday practical matters in a way that made little distinction between the natural and the supernatural.

Native Americans had a reverent and holistic (all-embracing) view of the world, considering themselves part of nature. Magic and mystery were inseparable from practical science, and both were explained through the myths and legends that were conceived as a way of understanding reality.

Sacred objects, music, dance, and personal humility and sacrifice to gain favor with the spirits were part of everyday life for Native Americans. And through ritual and ceremony, they related directly to the idea of medicine power as a mysterious force.

The source of all power

Many tribes believed this power came from a single and often unnameable and unknowable spirit source. The Algonquian groups knew this power as Manitou, the Iroquois called it Orenda, and the Sioux named it Wakonda. This power was the Great Medicine, or Great Mystery, or Mysterious One, from which everything, including people, derives motivation, reason, strength, and belief. It was the source of all power invested in people and in the spirits or ghosts of dead ancestors, in animals and plants, and in natural phenomena such as the sun and rain. It was possessed in equal amounts by guardian spirits, such as the kachinas of the Southwest, and demons, like the Algonquian windigos believed to haunt the Subarctic wastelands.

To the European colonists—despite their own beliefs in a large number of saints and demons possessing magical or miraculous powers—this was all superstitious paganism. Shamans were accordingly seen as the main barrier to wiping out Native American culture and converting Native Americans to

Windigo

An evil, greedy, but always hungry, cannibalistic spirit in Algonquian mythology, which could possess people or turn them into windigos, and make them eat human flesh.

Paganism

Religious belief in many gods or spirits.

Christianity. The Spanish, French, and English not only sent armies to the Americas to wage war, they sent missionaries to discredit the beliefs of the shamans.

Defending their beliefs

These attempts often met with strong resistance. The Pueblo Rebellion of 1680 was a response to brutal religious suppression, and the pan-Indian movements against colonialism led by Tecumseh, Pontiac, and Black Hawk in the late 18th and early 19th centuries were inspired by "prophets" preaching a return to the old medicine ways. Even the famous Sioux warrior Sitting Bull and Geronimo, the famous Apache resistance leader, were shamans, not military leaders.

Today, medicine power continues to be a source of strength for many Native Americans and is rapidly gaining a following among a broad cross-section of other people.

Pueblo Rebellion

A planned uprising of Pueblo peoples against Spanish colonization in August 1680. Many Spanish settlers and Franciscan priests were killed, and the Spanish fled from the city of Santa Fe.

A Navajo shaman, or medicine man, photographed in 1915. A shaman was both a leader of his people and a healer of the sick.

Modoc War

The Modoc people of what is now northern California and southern Oregon were involved in a number of violent clashes with white settlers from the 1850s onward. In 1864, the Modoc and the related Klamath people of southern Oregon made a treaty with the United States, by which they gave up much of their land and agreed to move to a reservation in southern Oregon.

However, the Modoc and Klamath did not get along together, and life on the reservation became intolerable for many Modoc people. Led by Kintpuash, a band of Modoc left the reservation to return to their former home in the Lost River area near Tule Lake, where they lived for several years. In 1869, they were persuaded to return to the reservation, but they stayed for only a few months before leaving once again.

Bureau of Indian Affairs

A U.S. federal government agency, formed in 1824, that administers land held in trust by the United States for Native Americans.

Late in 1872, the Bureau of Indian Affairs decided that Kintpuash and his followers must be forced to return to the reservation. In November, soldiers arrived in Kintpuash's camp to do just that. A fight broke out, and one soldier and one Modoc were killed. Not long before this happened, another Modoc band had clashed with white civilian vigilantes, killing 15 of them. This band united with Kintpuash and his people. Together, the Modoc took refuge in the area near Tule Lake, now called Lava Beds National Monument. They had a fighting force of only about 60 people, but the barren, jagged, and twisted landscape of the lava beds provided excellent defensive positions.

Sniper

Someone who shoots at an enemy while remaining hidden.

The beginning of the war

In January 1873, the U.S. Army tried to expel the Modoc. Over 300 soldiers, backed by an artillery barrage, moved toward Kintpuash and his men. About 40 of the soldiers were killed or wounded by Modoc snipers before the attack was called off.

Kintpuash realized it was time to negotiate and make the best deal he could. He told the army commander, General Edward Canby, that his people wanted only to be allowed to live among the lava beds, pointing out that these were valueless to the white settlers. General Canby could not agree to this, however, because it would have meant conceding victory to the Modoc, and the talks broke up at that point.

Another meeting was arranged for April 11, 1873. Kintpuash thought he could persuade General Canby to change his mind, but other Modoc warriors wanted Kintpuash to kill the general as a warning to the army to stay away. Kintpuash predicted that killing General Canby would only make the army so angry that they would crush the Modoc completely. Most of his people disagreed, however, so when the meeting took place, Kintpuash duly shot dead General Canby.

The army now sent in more than 1,000 men against the tiny force of Modoc. Despite massive attacks, backed by ferocious artillery fire, the Modoc were not immediately defeated. Instead, they picked off their white attackers almost at will. In late April, they ambushed a detachment of about 70 men, killing or wounding more than half of them.

Delaying the inevitable

The Modoc were running out of food and water and knew that they could not go on fighting forever. By the end of May 1873, many had surrendered. Kintpuash was among the last to give up, at the start of June. He and three other leaders were tried and hanged for the murder of General Canby.

The few surviving Modoc were shipped to a reservation in the Indian Territory, but some of their descendants were allowed to return to the Klamath reservation in 1909.

Indian Territory

Land mainly in present-day Oklahoma set aside in 1834 for Native Americans who had been forced to leave their homelands. The Indian Territory was dissolved when Oklahoma became a state in 1907.

Nez Percé War

In 1876, the U.S. Army was ordered to force some of the Nez Percé to move onto the Lapwai reservation in Idaho. When it became clear that the only option was war, Chief Joseph and other Nez Percé leaders agreed to move at the end of May 1877.

While the Nez Percé were moving to the reservation, a few young warriors, some of whose relatives had been murdered by settlers, carried out a number of revenge killings. An army detachment of 100 men and a group of civilian volunteers went to investigate the crime. Some Nez Percé came to meet them, carrying a white flag. However, the civilian settlers opened fire on the peace party. In the battle that followed, one-third of the soldiers were killed but only three Nez Percé were wounded. Fearing government retaliation, the Nez Percé fled the reservation under Chief Joseph. About 250 warriors and 500 women, children, and elderly people set out. They were pursued by about 2,000 U.S. Army troops under General Howard.

Escape from the army

The Nez Percé had to get away from the pursuing U.S. troops. In the early days of their retreat, they tried to pay white settlers for the supplies they needed. However, a series of battles occurred between the Nez Percé and the pursuing U.S. forces, notably at White Bird, Clearwater Creek, Big Hole, and Camas Creek. In each case, the Nez Percé outmaneuvered the army.

The Nez Percé tried to find a refuge with the Crow but were turned away, because the Crow did not wish to anger the U.S. authorities. Joseph and the other Nez Percé chiefs then decided to make for Canada.

The end of the flight

Another force of troops under Colonel Sturgis now left Fort Keogh to pursue the Nez Percé. By late September, the Nez Percé had reached the Bear Paw Mountains area of northern Montana, only 30 miles (45 km) from the Canadian border. They thought they had left the army far behind and stopped to hunt for food and to give their sick and wounded time to rest and recover.

However, they did not realize that General Howard had telegraphed ahead to arrange for more troops from Fort Keogh, under Colonel Miles, to block the escape to the border. These troops caught up with the tribe. A long battle raged, during which many Nez Percé died.

After six days of fighting, Chief Joseph knew that there was no alternative but to surrender. He sent a message to General Howard saying, "From where the sun now stands, I will fight no more forever." About 400 Nez Percé surrendered with Chief Joseph—another 150 managed to reach Canada. The tribe had repeatedly outsmarted the U.S. Army during their arduous journey. Today, the Nez Percé War is seen as a truly impressive military campaign.

The Nez Percé made a remarkable retreat of 1,700 miles (2,735 km) in three months during 1877. This map shows their journey in yellow, from the Lapwai reservation almost to the Canadian border, along with the battles they fought on the way.

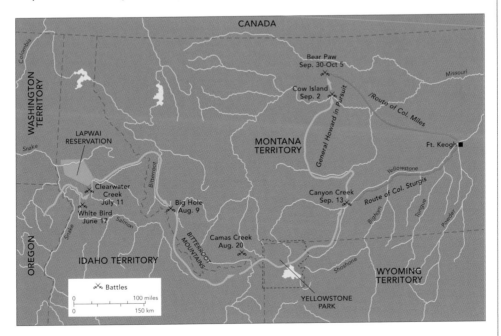

Pequot War

The Pequot War of 1636–1637 was the first major conflict fought between the New England settlers and Native Americans. The Pequot were part of an alliance of tribes who lived mainly in what today is known as Connecticut. They were feared by most other Native Americans in the region because of wars they had fought against them.

Trouble began in 1633 when a disreputable English sea captain called John Stone was killed by members of the Niantic people, who were allies of the Pequot. Despite Stone's character, the English of the Massachusetts Bay Colony were angry at his death and blamed the Pequot. The Pequot agreed to pay compensation and hand over the killers.

Colonist aggression

However, by 1636, this agreement had still not been fulfilled. Moreover, Uncas, the head of a breakaway Mohegan faction, warned the colonists that the Pequot were planning an attack. The colonists decided to act. Captain John Endecott led a force of about 100 men to Block Island, killing every male Native American they found and burning the villages. Endecott and his men then sailed along the Connecticut coast, fighting with Native Americans near the Pequot River. Enraged, the Pequot readied themselves for war.

War with the colonists

For the rest of 1636 and the spring of 1637, the Pequot besieged Fort Saybrook and attacked other local settlements. In one skirmish at Wethersfield, they killed nine settlers. The frightened English colonists decided to work together to defeat the Pequot.

In May 1637, Captain John Mason left Hartford with about 100 New Englanders, along with Niantic and

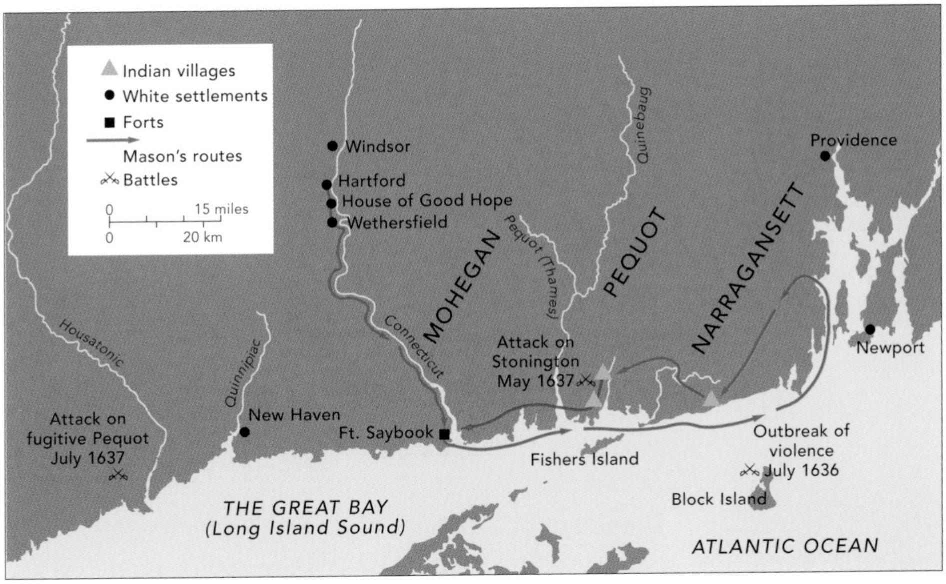
Indian villages
White settlements
Forts
Mason's routes
Battles
0 15 miles
0 20 km
Windsor
Hartford
House of Good Hope
Wethersfield
Providence
Quinebaug
Pequot (Thames)
MOHEGAN
PEQUOT
NARRAGANSETT
Housatonic
Connecticut
Quinnipiac
Attack on Stonington May 1637
Newport
Attack on fugitive Pequot July 1637
New Haven
Ft. Saybook
Fishers Island
Outbreak of violence July 1636
Block Island
THE GREAT BAY (Long Island Sound)
ATLANTIC OCEAN

This map shows the major battles between the Pequot and English colonists during the Pequot War of 1636–1637.

Narragansett allies, to attack the Pequot. They attacked a large Pequot village near present-day Stonington on May 25, 1637, setting light to the native houses. As the Pequot fled, a massacre began, and between 600 and 1,000 Pequot were killed. Other groups of Pequot were also defeated in a series of battles over the next two months.

End of the Pequot

In the end, the Pequot tribe was virtually wiped out. Many were captured and became slaves. Most of those remaining were absorbed into other tribes. The English banned the use of the Pequot tribal name, and Pequot place names were abolished. This once-proud people and their culture had been wholly destroyed.

Peyote

Peyote is a cactus that grows in northern Mexico and in the Rio Grande Valley in the Southwest. It contains mescaline, a nonaddictive drug that induces hallucinations, or visions, and a feeling of well-being.

Ghost Dance

A Native American religious movement of the late 19th century that involved the performance of a ritual dance, which, it was believed, would bring an end to the westward expansion of whites and restore land and traditional tribal life to Native Americans.

American Indian Religious Freedom Act

This law pledged to protect and preserve the traditional religious rights of Native Americans and stopped other laws from interfering with their religious practices. It allowed Native Americans access to their sacred places and to take part in ceremonies in private.

Mexican peoples and Apache who traveled into Mexico used peyote to put them in closer contact with the spirit world. The Comanche later adopted it as a ritual preparation for war and introduced it to their allies, the Kiowa, Cheyenne, and Arapaho.

The use of peyote became widespread after 1890, when the Ghost Dance movement, which promised salvation, collapsed following the massacre at Wounded Knee. Many Native Americans turned to peyote for temporary relief from their worries.

Its use was encouraged by the Comanche leader Quanah Parker, resulting in the foundation of an organized peyote religion that included members of many peoples: the Native American Church. Its ceremonies were led by a Road Man, who taught people to follow the Peyote Road to help them live together and support one another.

Banned—then allowed

Many U.S. states, claiming peyote was dangerous, banned its use by the Native American Church. But the church grew rapidly and, in 1918, Oklahoma authorized the use of peyote by the church. About half the Native American population of Oklahoma, plus many Native Americans in other states, joined the church, which in 1930 was recognized by the Bureau of Indian Affairs. Even so, some states banned the church from using peyote. But in 1978, the U.S. government prevented states' banning peyote when it passed the American Indian Religious Freedom Act.

Pontiac's War

The conflict known as Pontiac's War was fought between the British and a coalition of Native American peoples, including the Ottawa, Delaware, Seneca, and Shawnee. Pontiac was an Ottawa chief, but although the war is known by his name, he was only one of several important Native American leaders involved.

The British first garrisoned Fort Detroit in 1760 during the French and Indian War. Pontiac knew that the French defeat would lead to the arrival of more British settlers in the Ohio and Great Lakes region.

In 1761, the British commander-in-chief, General Jeffrey Amherst, stopped giving the Native Americans guns and ammunition. This limited the Native Americans' ability to fight and—because they now relied on guns for hunting— meant they would starve.

The battle for the forts

The Ottawa and other tribes made plans to attack the British forts in 1761 and again in 1762, but they came to nothing. In May 1763, Pontiac led attacks on Fort Detroit. His first plan was to make a surprise attack, but he called it off when he realized that the garrison was on the alert. Pontiac and his people had to settle for a five-month siege of the fort. The fort held out easily.

Other British forts did not fare so well. At least eight were captured and destroyed during May and June, and almost all of the troops in them were killed. Many forts were taken by surprise. In one instance, some Ojibway staged a lacrosse game outside Fort Michilimackinac in Michigan that was watched by the garrison. At one point, the ball "accidentally" landed in the fort. The players ran after it, produced weapons that they had concealed beneath their clothing, and attacked the soldiers.

French and Indian War

A war (1754–1763) fought between Britain and France and their respective native allies for colonial supremacy in North America. British victory was confirmed in the Treaty of Paris in 1763.

Lacrosse

A Native American ball game, played with sticks or rackets, in which two teams attempt to land a ball in each other's goal. There are several widely differing versions of the game, which was also used to settle disputes and conflicts.

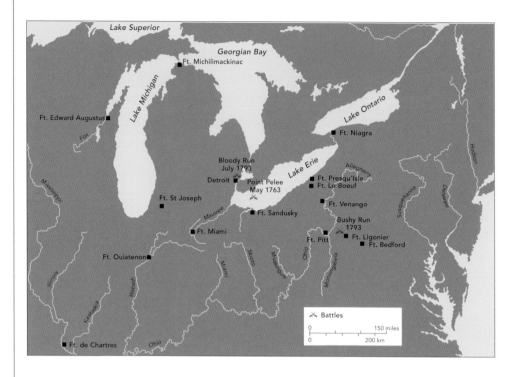

This map indicates the major battles of Pontiac's War.

Fort Pitt and others in Pennsylvania held out. The commander of Fort Pitt met with the Delaware for a truce and gave them blankets as presents. However, the blankets had been infected with the disease smallpox, and the Delaware were soon dying from it.

There were three big battles during the war: Bloody Run, Point Pelee, and Bushy Run, which was fought on August 5 and 6, when a 500-strong relief expedition was attacked on their way to Fort Pitt. Fifty men were killed on both sides during the two days of fighting.

An end to the rebellion

In October, Pontiac agreed to a peace. A few days later, the British issued the Royal Proclamation, forbidding white settlement west of the Appalachian Mountains.

Some Native Americans fought on, but almost all had made peace by the fall of 1764. About 2,500 whites died during the war, 500 of them soldiers. No one knows how many Native Americans died.

Royal Proclamation

This British order of King George III in 1763 set aside the Indian Reserve, mainly made up of land in Louisiana and Canada taken from the French, for use by Native Americans.

Population Density

Native American population densities in all areas of North America have changed dramatically since Europeans began colonizing the continent. Estimates of the total population before then vary from as low as two million to as high as 10 million.

The most populous area was California. Its mild climate attracted peoples from many different language groups. There were also large populations in the Woodland areas. In the Southwest, people were concentrated in pueblo villages; few people lived in the desert. Hardly anyone lived in the Arctic and Subarctic. The Great Plains also had relatively few inhabitants.

European wars, settlement, and epidemics changed Native American populations dramatically. Most of the Californian peoples were wiped out, and those of the Woodlands suffered a drastic loss in numbers. In the 19th century, U.S. government policies forcibly moved many peoples out of their homelands. The Indian Territory (now Oklahoma) became a center for them, even though few people had lived there before.

Moving to find work

Further changes in Native American numbers and densities occurred in the 20th century. Many people left their reservations in the 1950s and 1960s to find work in the cities, partly because conditions on the reservations were poor, with low incomes and low living standards. The relocation was encouraged by U.S. officials, who felt that the quickest way to make Native Americans conform to white American society was to persuade them to move away from their reservations.

Curriculum Context

Students can explore the extent to which native American poverty today is the result of 19th-century federal policies.

Today, about half of all Native Americans live in urban communities. There they do seasonal or temporary work, returning to their reservations only for tribal ceremonies. Los Angeles has the highest Native

This map shows the main areas of relatively low, moderate, and high population densities in North America before the arrival of the first Europeans in the early 16th century.

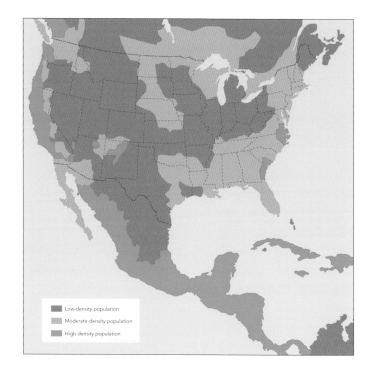

Low-density population

Moderate-density population

High-density population

American population, at 100,000. Next is Chicago, followed by Minneapolis–St. Paul, Oklahoma City, New York City, San Francisco, Seattle, and Phoenix.

Census

A government-organized count of the total population of a country.

Most estimates of the Native American population today come from the U.S. census, which records only people who live on reservations or have Indian Status. Indian Status depends on how much Native American blood someone inherits from his or her parents, but tribes have different rules about this. Other estimates are based on the number of people on tribal rolls— those who can claim membership on a reservation.

Increase and decrease

The Native American population of North America today probably totals about five million, but few are "full-bloods." In recent times, a few tribes, such as the Navajo, Ojibway (Chippewa), and Pima and Papago, have grown in number, mainly because of people marrying into them. Other tribes are getting smaller.

Pottery

Evidence suggests that the craft of pottery was widespread among Native Americans in Pre-Contact times, except for peoples in the far north, the Northwest Coast, and parts of California and the Columbia Plateau.

The principal pottery regions were the Southwest and the Eastern Woodlands. In both, pots were made with either coiling or modeling techniques. In coiling, characteristic of the Southwest, rolls of clay are added to a base and pinched together as the pot is shaped. In modeling, a flat "pancake" of clay is inverted over a mold. Modeled pots are often finished and enlarged by adding coils of clay once the base has been completed.

Pottery techniques

Pots were decorated using a variety of techniques. In negative style, the background rather than the foreground elements is painted first; the reverse is the case for positive style. In the "corrugated style," ridges of coils are prominent on the outside of the pot. Other styles included incising, engraving, and stamping. Stamps were made of cord-wrapped tools or pieces of shell, bone, and other materials that had been shaped.

Cord-marked, incised, and stamped designs are familiar from eastern prehistoric pottery and were used by several peoples, such as the Iroquois, Huron, Delaware, Cherokee, Creek, Choctaw, Caddo, and Natchez. Middle Mississippian cultures modeled clay-head pots depicting the severed heads of captives as well as hunchbacked female figures. They also produced a considerable quantity of finely worked animal effigies, often as bowls for tobacco pipes.

Effigy
An image or representation of a person or animal.

Most of these techniques had died out by the mid-18th century. By then, potware had generally been replaced by European goods. A few tribes, such as the Iroquois and Seminole, continued to make pots into the modern period.

Pottery in the Southwest

The Southwest is the only area where Native Americans still make traditional pottery. There, pottery-making goes back to the Mogollon and Hohokam cultures, which date from around 100 BCE. Pueblo pots are from an Anasazi tradition, developed after 700 CE, that reached its peak at Mesa Verde, Chaco, and Kayenta. Although they share a common tradition, the modern Pueblo have evolved their own individual styles.

The finest pottery is produced at Acoma and is characterized by very thin-walled and carefully painted pots with geometric motifs on a white-to-cream backing. Acoma craftworkers base many of their designs on prehistoric patterns used by the Anasazi.

Fine pottery is also made at Zuni, with brown-black designs on a chalk-white background, although the pots tend to be heavier than those from Acoma. A relatively recent trend is the production of small figurines, often of owls, which are fashioned from clay and painted in commercial colors for the tourist trade.

Similar figurines, known as "story-tellers" or "singing mothers" because they often feature mothers with their children, have become a distinct type of Pueblo folk art since 1964. Those from Cochiti are best known. The potters there also make a variety of humorous figurines of frogs and other animals. These, again, are produced for sale and painted in commercial colors, as is much of the pottery produced at Tesuque.

Pueblo styles

Other Pueblo sites have also developed distinctive, contemporary styles. The most famous is San Ildefonso. Here, in 1919, Maria and Julian Martinez introduced a technique using polished black designs on a matte black background. Martinez pottery is now sought by collectors, but craftworkers at San Ildefonso and at Santa Clara produce work in this style for general sale.

A few Pueblo villages, such as Zia and Santo Domingo, continue to make limited amounts of pottery for sale. Pottery from Taos and Picuris tends to be sought after for kitchen use rather than display. Potters at Taos and Picuris use a clay tempered with mica, which gives a gold-tan glitter to the finished product.

This Hopi potter decorating pots in a Pueblo style was photographed more than a century ago; since then, newer Pueblo designs have been developed.

Other Southwest styles

Final mention needs to be made of peoples living near the Pueblo. The Maricopa are known for their finely made bowls and jars with a highly polished red gloss. In contrast, the Yuma and Mohave are known historically for the manufacture of pottery dolls, although few of these, if any, are made today. Pima, Papago, and Navajo pots are produced in very limited quantities; those of the Pima and Papago are red polished ware with black designs, often in the form of water ollas, or jars. Navajo pottery is relatively crude and limited to utility cookware.

Poverty

Poverty is the condition of lacking the quality of food, housing, and opportunity needed for individuals to live comfortably according to socially accepted standards. Poverty has been forced on Native Americans by historical circumstances and because both the public and the government have, until recently, remained largely indifferent to the realities of Native American life.

Curriculum Context

Some curricula ask students to make comparisons between European and Native American exploitation of natural resources.

From a historical perspective, native poverty is regarded as beginning with the first contacts with European colonists. The Europeans' beliefs, attitudes, social institutions, and material needs were very different from those of native peoples. Although the settlers came from many different cultures, they shared one aim: to exploit the "New World's" resources and lands for themselves, without any thought for the needs of Native Americans.

Integration

The destructive effects of the colonists' desire for land were intensified by United States and Canadian government policies of "assimilation" or "integration." Such policies have always removed Native Americans from their lands and thus made it harder for them to hunt and gather food. At the same time, these policies undermined tribal identity and created dependence on government funding.

Government attempts at self-help and assimilation have often increased social discrimination and made it harder for Native Americans to find jobs. They have faced such difficulties as unproductive land with inadequate resources to improve it, unemployment that can be as high as 70 percent, and associated problems of social isolation. These problems have all combined to create a cycle of deprivation that has proved difficult to break.

Life in the cities

For many Native Americans, cities have offered better housing, education, and job prospects than has reservation life. Since the 1970s, 50 percent of United States Native Americans have moved to cities, while in Canada the figure is 30 percent.

Reservation life

Although there is a strong sense of community on reservations, it alone cannot solve the problems of Native Americans. On some reservations there can be extreme poverty. Few native communities have enough money to set up their own aid programs. In order to survive, tribes and individuals are frequently forced to sell or lease land and mineral rights. This undermines their independence and makes them reliant on outsiders, who may have little concern for native interests and priorities.

However, city life has tended to increase isolation for Native Americans, often more than for other ethnic groups. In the United States, Native Americans have the shortest life span of any ethnic minority, the highest suicide rate, the lowest income per person, the highest unemployment rate, and the poorest housing. The situation in Canada is little better; about half of Native Canadians depend on social assistance for survival, and with over half the native population lacking running water and sewage-disposal facilities.

New developments

Without adequate land and resources, there is little native groups can do to combat poverty or improve their lives. Although, in theory, several peoples were given government money in treaty agreements, much of it is in trust accounts with little direct native access. Federal funding, too, is difficult to obtain and is growing smaller. The total funding available now is less than half of 1 percent of the federal budget.

Curriculum Context

The U.S. government's historic policies on land ownership, reservation creation, and assimilation have caused many of the problems Native Americans face today.

However, new initiatives and self-help groups, including a number of urban social centers, are providing support to disadvantaged Native Americans. They are also encouraging an awareness of and pride in a native identity. The younger generation, too, is realizing the values of retaining community ideals and is returning to reservations from urban centers for at least a part of each year.

Heirloom

Something of value handed from one generation to the next.

Short-term measures to combat poverty, such as the sale of family heirlooms to collectors and dealers in Native American art, are gradually being discouraged, allowing increasing numbers of young craftworkers to become self-sufficient in the craft market.

Peoples are becoming more aware of the need to conserve their land and to manage their financial resources. Native American business councils that oversee investment funding and hire outside consultants are being created.

Although the problems of poverty remain severe at both tribal and individual levels, there are programs and organizations emphasizing positive attitudes and encouraging pride in a Native American heritage. International awareness of the problems faced by ethnic minority communities is also on the increase.

Powhatan Wars

The Powhatan Wars were fought in 1622–1632 and 1644–1646 between the Powhatan confederacy of Algonquian peoples and the English colonists of Jamestown in Virginia. Jamestown was established in 1607 and became the first permanent English settlement in what is now the United States.

The colony maintained a fragile truce with the Powhatan, their leader Chief Powhatan, and his daughter, Pocahontas. Powhatan died in 1618, and his successor, Opechancano, was more hostile.

War breaks out

In 1622, one of the English colonists disappeared. His friends captured and killed a Native American in revenge. On March 22, Opechancano attacked the settlement, killing 347 of the colony's 1,200 people.

The fighting continued on and off for about 10 years. Cruel and brutal acts were committed by both sides. On one occasion, the colonists served poisoned food to Opechancano and other leaders who had come to negotiate a truce. Opechancano survived, but others died. In the fall of 1632, a truce was signed with the colonists that finally brought the fighting to an end.

The last battle

In 1644, Opechancano decided to attack again. About 500 colonists were killed in the early stages of the fighting. By then, however, the colonial population had grown to over 8,000, and they were able to fight back.

In 1646, Opechancano was captured and killed, and his successor, Necotowance, made a new treaty with the English. This treaty allocated land exclusively to Necotowance and the Powhatan, but it was not respected for long.

Curriculum Context

When studying the relationships between Native Americans and early English settlers, it is useful to compare the Powhatan Wars in Virginia with the Pequot War in Massachusetts Bay.

Queen Anne's War

Queen Anne's War was named for the British Queen Anne (r.1702–1714) and was part of a larger European conflict known as the War of the Spanish Succession. Spain, France, and their colonies in Canada, Louisiana, and Florida were on one side, and Britain and other European countries and their North American colonies were on the other. The war began in Europe in 1701, but fighting did not begin in North America until 1702.

Raids and reprisals

There were no large-scale battles. There was, instead, a long series of brutal raids, murders, and reprisals that ultimately benefited no one. Native Americans became involved in the fighting because of the trade alliances they had with the Europeans in North America.

Native Americans took part in the war in Florida and New England. The first fighting was an attack in 1702 by a colonial force from South Carolina on the Spanish fort at Saint Augustine, Florida. In the next two years, the Carolinians, aided by Chickasaw warriors, made repeated attacks on settlements in the Apalachee area of western Florida, destroying most villages and almost wiping out the Apalachee. Attempts by the British to push on into France's small colony in Louisiana were blocked by the Choctaw—allies of the French.

In New England, there were many raids on colonial settlements by Abenaki people and others. Deerfield, in modern-day Massachusetts, was hard hit in an attack in February 1704. French and Native Americans also captured British settlements in Newfoundland.

The Treaty of Utrecht ended the war in 1713 and gave Britain control of Acadia, and of territory around Hudson Bay. Once again, Native Americans had lost out by being drawn into a European conflict.

Acadia

The French name for their lands in northeastern North America that included parts of eastern Quebec, New Brunswick, Nova Scotia, Prince Edward Island, and New England.

Salmon

Salmon was a vital food for Native Americans living on the Northwest Coast. Every summer, huge numbers of salmon battle the rapids and waterfalls of the fast-flowing major rivers of the region to reach their spawning grounds.

Native Americans living on these Northwest rivers caught salmon in great numbers. Excess fish was dried, smoked, and stored to sustain the people in winter and to provide food for the lavish feasts during *tsetseka*—the winter ceremonial season.

The reliability of salmon as a food source enabled Northwest Coast peoples, such as the Tlingit, Coast Salish, Chinook, and Haida, to lead a settled life and construct large winter villages.

Salmon rituals

The importance of salmon in their daily lives led Northwest Coast peoples to believe that the fish had supernatural powers, and they built a number of mythological stories around it. Tales of the First Salmon, called "older brother," were common, as were First Salmon Rites celebrating the return of the salmon to the rivers each year. During these rituals, the tribes blessed the first salmon caught and returned its bones to the river, so that the fish might carry with it the good wishes of the people. The ceremony is still practiced today.

The Hupa people built this weir across the Trinity River in California to help them catch salmon as the fish migrated upriver to their spawning grounds.

Scalping

Scalping is the removal of hair and skin from the head of an enemy. It was widely practiced in North America, especially among tribes of the Great Plains. Current opinion is that scalping was known to Native Americans before Europeans arrived.

Curriculum Context

Students can compare the very different attitudes of Native Americans and Europeans to scalping.

What is certain is that Europeans began paying for native scalps, which made scalping a source of income for some settlers.

Honor or bounty

Native Americans believed that scalping was an honor paid to a defeated warrior who had fought bravely. By taking the scalp, they thought they captured the victim's soul, or spirit, which was said to reside in the hair. Native Americans believed the soul of the victim would then accompany the victor's soul in the afterlife—a great honor.

Although they all shared this belief in capturing the enemy's soul, attitudes among peoples varied widely. Most scalps were a small piece of hair taken from the crown of the head, inflicting a painful but not necessarily fatal wound. Some Siouan tribes took the entire head-hair and also parts of the face. In contrast, the Pima and Papago of the Southwest took only four hairs as a symbolic scalp and followed this with a 14-day purification rite. The Apache took no scalps at all.

Bounty

A payment for the capture or murder of a specified person or people.

Europeans, however, considered scalps as proof of a killing and paid bounties to anyone who brought back enemy scalps. Bounty hunters were encouraged to wipe out local peoples and free their lands for settlement. Men, women, and children were killed in the interests of European expansion, and their scalps were displayed to the public. Even during the 19th century, the states of Sonora and Chihuahua in Mexico were paying bounties for the scalps of dead Apache.

Scouts

The tracking skills of Native Americans were legendary and were made use of by hunters, explorers, trappers, and various military units from the start of the European presence in North America. In the 19th century, many U.S. Army units were able to locate the camps of their enemies only by using Native American scouts.

Uncanny abilities

Scouts could follow a trail over hard ground on which soldiers could see no marks at all. They were often able to say which group the tracks were made by, how many people were in the group, the direction it was moving in, and how long it had been since it had passed by.

Most scouts signed on for a limited period of service, usually six months. Most wore blue U.S. Army jackets and red headbands, so soldiers could tell they were friendly. They were led by chief scouts, who were usually whites the native people respected.

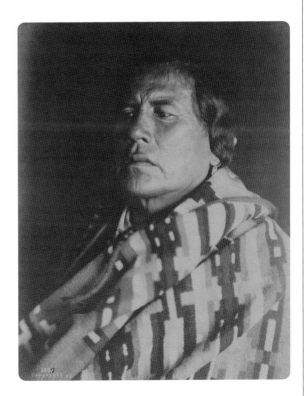

Although these scouts served the United States loyally, the government paid little regard to their service. At the end of hostilities, most scouts were imprisoned along with the hostile Native Americans they had helped track down.

This Native American scout worked for Lieutenant Colonel Custer and the 7th cavalry in the 1870s.

Shields

A Native American warrior's shield was a vital piece of war equipment, as it provided him with protection. Not only was his shield physically tough; in the warrior's mind, it also had supernatural qualities. Each warrior believed that his "medicine shield" contained the power of his guardian spirit, which would protect him from danger in battle.

Built to buffer blows

Native American shields were generally round. Plains warriors made shields by smoking or heating layers of buffalo skin to shrink them and then stretching them thin. They padded them with hair, feathers, grass, or even paper. According to George Catlin, an artist who traveled among the Native Americans in the 1830s, warriors of some Plains peoples further toughened their shields with glue made by boiling buffalo hooves. Plains shields were tough enough to stop an arrow or a blow from a tomahawk. Skillfully handled, they could deflect a round from a low-powered firearm.

A Plains warrior took great care of his shield. He believed he could recharge its protective power by placing it on a stand and pointing it toward the sun. He would not usually let it touch the ground. However, one 19th-century Plains chief, Arapooish of the Crow people, had a shield that he rolled along the ground to predict the result of a coming battle. If the shield landed face upward, then Arapooish believed his war party would win.

Warriors often kept their shields in highly decorated cases. A Plains warrior usually also decorated his shield with likenesses of his guardian, or vision, spirit. It was this decoration that gave the shield its supernatural protective power. So, if a warrior's guardian spirit was a buffalo, he might paint a buffalo's head on it.

When the Apache went to war, they tried to harness the powers of animal spirits that they revered. They sometimes painted pictures of these animals on their shields. One Apache shield, for example, bears images of a hummingbird, which the shield's owner believed could lend him its speed, and a bat, which he thought could pass on its ability to hide and be hard to catch.

From shields to symbols

Shields changed in size over the years. Before they acquired horses in the 18th century, Plains warriors carried shields that were about 3 feet (90 cm) across. However, shields this large were awkward on horseback, so Plains warriors changed to smaller ones, between 18 inches (45 cm) and 2 feet (60 cm) across.

The development of powerful firearms also influenced the size of Native American warriors' shields. Realizing that their shields could not physically protect them from gunfire, warriors began to carry small, symbolic shields into battle. Like their full-sized shields, they decorated these models with likenesses of their guardian spirits and believed that they had the same supernatural protective powers. Sometimes warriors carried only their shield cover or even a lacework shield into battle.

This Arapaho warrior, photographed around 1900, is holding a small, symbolic shield. By this time, shields had no defensive value in battle.

Tobacco

Tobacco is native to North America and was unknown in Europe until the English explorer Sir Walter Raleigh introduced it as a medicinal plant at the end of the 16th century. Smoking dried tobacco leaves or sniffing them in powder form as snuff quickly became popular among the nobility in France, Portugal, Spain, and England. By the mid-16th century, colonies such as Virginia generated a major part of their income from tobacco exports.

Native Americans rarely used tobacco socially. The variety they grew most, *Nicotiana rustica*, is a powerful stimulant. They used it mainly in ceremonies as an aid to establishing contact with the spirit world. Smoking tobacco "made the breath visible." Since breathing is the essence of life, tobacco smoke rising from Earth to the spiritual abode in the skies was seen as carrying their wishes and prayers heavenward.

Ceremonial crop

Tobacco was cultivated in all the farming areas of North America. Some peoples who planted no other crops sometimes grew it ceremonially. For example, when the Crow split from the farming Hidatsa and became nomadic buffalo hunters, they retained a tradition of planting sacred tobacco in fields tended by only the most highly respected male elders. Even among farming peoples, caring for the tobacco fields was seen as an honored occupation for men who had otherwise retired from active life as hunters and warriors.

Elder
Someone holding authority because of their age or experience.

There is archaeological evidence of widespread tobacco use in Pre-Contact North America. The Anasazi, Mogollon, and Hohokam of the Southwest all planted tobacco, and the Adena and Hopewell of the Woodlands and Southeast established a trade in tobacco and related products. Figurine pipes depicting humans and animals have been found at many Hopewell sites.

Native Americans used tobacco in every way familiar today, such as rolling and smoking it as cigarettes or chewing it. Most famously of all, they smoked it in pipes called calumets. Commonly called peace pipes because they were used to seal bonds of friendship and nonaggression, they were also used to communicate directly with the spirit powers at important ceremonies. Calumets had elaborately decorated stems, often covered with painted, quilled, or beaded hide and adorned with horsehair, cloth, beads, miniature flint arrowheads or shells, and fans made from the wing feathers of birds of prey.

Calumets probably originated in the East but soon became common among peoples along the Missouri and Mississippi rivers and on the Plains. Among the Blackfoot, for instance, calumet owners sealed pacts of friendship and led the way when the group moved camp, carrying the pipes to "clear the path."

It is said that any Native American entering a hostile camp with a pipe was welcomed and assured safe passage. Sharing pipes and offering guests tobacco are common customs still among Native Americans, and few ceremonies would be considered complete without their use.

Tobacco became important for the economic success of European settlers. It was grown on plantations in Virginia by slaves from Africa and made huge profits for the plantation owners.

Tomahawk

Tomahawks, or war axes, were traditional Native American weapons. Tomahawks could be held in the hand and used as hatchets, or they could be thrown. The word *tomahawk* comes from an Algonquian word meaning "to knock down."

Different styles

Early tomahawks were made of stone. The head could be ax-shaped or round and was bound tightly to a strong wooden shaft with tough animal sinew. Later, iron and steel weapons were acquired from white traders and adapted to make tomahawks. Some metal blades were single and hatchet-shaped or pointed like spearheads. Others were double blades with a hatchet on one side and a spike on the other.

Some wooden tomahawk handles were beautifully carved. Ceremonial tomahawks might be adorned with feathers. Tomahawks with hollow handles were tipped with an ax blade and a pipe bowl, and could be used both as a weapon and as a pipe for smoking tobacco.

Native Americans also used war clubs. Gun-stock clubs were shaped like the butt of a rifle and had a metal blade sunk into one edge. Other wooden clubs had a ball-shaped head into which a metal spike was set.

Some peoples ceremonially buried a tomahawk when they made peace with an enemy. This may have given rise to the modern expression "to bury the hatchet."

This painting of a Winnebago chief holding a tomahawk was painted in the 1840s. The Winnebago people live in Wisconsin, Illinois, Iowa, and Nebraska.

Trade

Native American trade patterns were well established in North America before European contact. Trade routes crisscrossed the continent—Adena and Hopewell traders traveled from the Woodland regions to virtually every corner of North America.

Trade between the Southeast, Southwest, and Mexico flourished. Trading links between Florida and Cuba were also strong. Peoples of the Plateau traded materials from the Pacific Coast to Great Plains groups. The Tlingit controlled trade routes into the interior from the coasts of British Columbia and Alaska and made trade voyages in seagoing canoes to California.

Most native trade was in goods and materials that could not be obtained locally and so were considered luxuries. Early colonial traders capitalized on exchanging European goods for native products, using preexisting native trade routes. White exploration of these trade routes contributed greatly to the opening of the so-called "wilderness" areas north of Mexico.

Trading with Europeans

European trade was started by the French in 1534 with Jacques Cartier's voyages along the St. Lawrence River and was expanded in 1603 by Samuel de Champlain. By 1672, the French had set up a trading company to compete with the English-owned Hudson's Bay Company. The English company had established its own charter and was granted a trading monopoly in Rupert's Land by the British Crown in 1670. It was so firmly associated with trading that ownership of "Bay" blankets became a standard measure of wealth in many northern regions.

European trade and exploration were fueled by a search for new sources of wealth and a desire to obtain power and prestige. Trading routes were improved

Curriculum Context

Some curricula include studies of Native American trading links and systems in Pre-Contact times.

Rupert's Land

The vast area of modern-day Canada from which rivers drain into Hudson Bay. It was owned by the Hudson's Bay Company from 1670 to 1870.

through better oceangoing ships, more advanced navigation techniques, and more accurate maps. The so-called "New World" offered unbounded opportunities for the satisfaction of European desires, as well as providing ample opportunities for those with a sense of adventure or a thirst for knowledge.

Although France and Britain were the major trade competitors in North America, other nations were also involved. The Spanish penetrated the continent from the south, via Mexico and Florida, while the Dutch expanded to the northwest along the Hudson River. Russian traders came from Siberia into Alaska and extended their activities south into California.

Wars and alliances

European rivalries in America resulted in dissent and conflict. During the French and Indian War of the mid-18th century, France and Britain both relied heavily on alliances with different peoples originally formed through trading agreements. Similarly, the colonies' decision to break away from Britain—the American Revolution, leading to the formation of the United States in 1776—was inspired by their refusal to pay tax to a remote English parliament where their interests were not represented.

Following independence, American and Canadian policy continued to favor peoples with whom profitable trade relationships could be maintained. It is true that European—and later American and Canadian—trade contacts were established on the basis of the needs of those nations. However, these contacts made the peoples with whom the Europeans dealt dependent on European goods and trade.

Reliance on Europeans

Firearms were preeminent among early European trade goods, since groups armed with them could establish

American Revolution

War fought (1775–1783) between Britain and the Revolutionaries, also known as Colonials or Patriots. Britain was defeated and most of the former British colonies in North America gained their independence to become the United States of America.

European goods

Other European trade goods quickly became a necessary part of everyday native life. They included metal-bladed tools and knives, copper and iron kettles, and trade cloth. However, numerous luxury items were also in regular demand; beads soon came to replace porcupine and bird quills in native decorative embroidery. Native Americans also began to use manufactured dyes and paints in place of traditional natural colors derived from minerals and other sources.

superiority over those armed only with native weapons. But guns required ammunition, which was obtainable only from Europeans. In this way, a cycle was created in which Native Americans had no option but to trade with Europeans.

Changing culture

Traded items were so important they completely changed many native cultures. For example, 19th-century Plains culture relied heavily on two items introduced by Europeans: the horse and the gun. They were obtained from trading with Anglo-Americans or acquired through trading with other Native American groups (or raiding them).

The Cree of the Subarctic became dependent on iron traps for hunting, both to secure meat to eat and to get furs to trade. On the Northwest Coast, the massive cedar-wood carvings called totem poles developed from smaller carved house-posts only after metal tools replaced earlier bone and shell tools.

For many native groups, their primary relationship with settlers was through the itinerant (traveling) trader or the trading post. Today, the trading post continues to be a symbol of this relationship as well as a major source of income for many Native American families— either through employment with trading companies or from the sale of artifacts to tourists.

Curriculum Context

It is important for students to understand that Native American–European trade in horses, guns, and metal objects transformed the lifestyles of many native peoples and that guns in particular also influenced later events.

Totem poles

Sculptures carved from large trees by tribes of the Northwest Coast. The designs illustrate legends or important events, clan lineages, or shamanic powers.

Travois

Native American people did not use the wheel. They had no carts, wagons, or any other type of wheeled vehicle, although we know that the concept of the wheel was familiar to them. Children in Mesoamerica (central Mexico to Nicaragua) often played with wheeled toys, and many wheeled and hooped forms were used in ceremonies throughout North America.

One possible reason why Native Americans did not use the wheel might be that they viewed it as a symbol of life and therefore as too sacred an emblem to be used for everyday tasks.

Even in relatively recent periods, most Native Americans traveled by foot, and they manufactured a countless variety of packs, baskets, jars, and other containers that could be carried comfortably.

Pulled by dogs
However, the nomadic lifestyle of the Great Plains, where whole tribes moved constantly, gave rise to the travois. It was an A-shaped frame with a closed end that originally fitted over the shoulders of large domesticated dogs that pulled the frame. The free end was left to trail along the ground. A platform on the travois was used to store bundles of belongings, tepee coverings, and other goods.

Adaptability of the travois
In the 16th century, the Spanish brought horses to North America, and Plains people adapted the travois to fit them. The greater size and strength of a horse compared to a dog meant that native peoples could now transport larger loads. Use of the horse travois made it possible for them to acquire some luxury goods and nonessentials that had previously been too difficult to carry.

The horse travois also caused changes in social practice, since it could be used for carrying the elderly, sick, or frail. This development ended the practice of abandoning those who were unable to keep up with the rapid movements of the tribe as it followed migrating game animals.

Travois and tepees

Large tepees required long poles, which were often ingeniously used as a makeshift travois frame. Bundles of tepee poles were lashed to either side of a horse, and a spacer bar was used to maintain the A-shape of the frame and to spread the trailing ends of the poles. In this way, a family was able to move greater quantities of goods and larger homes.

Rugged terrain

Another advantage of the travois was that it could be used on narrow or rutted paths and trails that were impassable to wagons. During the Plains Indian Wars, one of the reasons that the Native Americans could move so rapidly, and therefore evade pursuit, was their ability to use narrow tracks and passes. U.S. troops, who were dependent on bulky supply wagons, found it difficult to follow them.

The travois was so adaptable for use in rugged country that it was adopted as a means of transportation by many French Canadians. It was also widely used during the early days of the logging industry.

Gros Ventres families set out on a journey with horse-pulled travois in this photo taken in 1908. The Gros Ventres were traditionally a people of the Canadian Prairies, who were forced to move south and adopt Plains culture.

Wampum

The Algonquian word *wampum* has entered the English language as slang for "money." But for both the Iroquois and the Algonquian, it had many uses and meanings. A wampum is a string of beads that were originally made by grinding down purple and white clamshells.

Wampums were used as currency and worn as belts, necklaces, or bracelets. Certain lengths of wampum had specific values, although purple beads were considered to be twice as valuable as white ones.

Ceremony and event-marker

As well as being used for currency, wampums featured prominently in ceremonies. The value of the wampum was related to the richness of the ritual. Wampum was also widely used to maintain a tribal record of agreements. When, for example, the separate Iroquois tribes consolidated and formed the Iroquois League of Nations, the event was recorded in symbols on a wampum belt. The belt was held by the Onondaga, the Keepers of the Central Fire, where council meetings of the league were held and where important intertribal decisions were made. Similarly, the agreements made with the Iroquois by William Penn, an English Quaker who founded Pennsylvania, were recorded on a wampum belt.

Wampum belts also functioned as a means of communication between different tribal groups or factions. After the defeat of the French forces in the Great Lakes region, Lord Jeffrey Amherst, the British commander-in-chief, granted Seneca tribal lands to his British officers in reward for their services. The Seneca chiefs sent out war belts of wampum to enlist the help of neighboring tribes against the British forces. The act was a precursor to Pontiac's War of 1763.

Iroquois League of Nations

A league of Native American peoples of the northeastern United States that was founded well before Europeans arrived in the Americas, possibly as early as the 12th century. These peoples were the Mohawk, Oneida, Onondaga, Cayuga, and Seneca, and later, the Tuscarora.

War Costumes

Plains warriors wore little clothing when fighting but during ceremonies, they put on highly decorated war costumes that indicated their status as successful fighters. The decorations allowed everyone to see how important the warrior was.

Markings and meaning

A typical Plains war costume featured deerskin or sheepskin leggings and a war shirt. Both leggings and war shirts, also called scalp shirts, often bore coded markings that signified battle honors. On one well-preserved Blackfoot scalp shirt, for example, honors are represented by painted stripes on the shoulders. Pipes and arrows painted over the stripes show that the owner had led war parties, while painted hoofmarks represent the horses he had captured. A fringe of human hair hanging from the shoulders of the shirt represents enemies he had killed.

The leggings also feature painted stripes—showing the owner was an important warrior—and are fringed with human hair and horse hair.

Honors and protection

A warrior's battle record could be shown on his shirt by bands or rosettes of beads or quills. Some shirts also featured painted marks showing old war wounds. A warrior's scalp shirt might carry likenesses of his vision spirit to ensure he received supernatural protection. In addition, black tadpolelike shapes on a scalp shirt were thought to protect the wearer against firearms.

Chief Umapine of the Cayuse, a people in Oregon, dressed in full ceremonial costume in 1909.

Over the top of his shirt, a warrior might also wear a buffalo-skin or wolf-skin robe. This garment could also describe a war record and was sometimes decorated with scenes depicting heroic episodes from the warrior's career.

On his feet, a warrior wore animal skin moccasins. These were highly decorated and showed information about the wearer. For example, some Mandan warriors wore moccasins with wolf tails attached to their heels. This signified that the wearer was a scout.

Headdresses for heroes

Some Plains warriors wore breastplates made of hollow tubes or hair pipes (thin rods of shell or the wing bones of birds). Others, such as the Sioux and Hidatsa, wore cut and marked feathers in their hair—a code showing the wearer's war honors. In addition, the Arikara and the Mandan also put painted sticks or painted wooden weapons in their hair to display war honors. Very brave Plains warriors wore flowing feather war bonnets.

Strings of bear claws were worn around the neck by some groups as the sign of an accomplished fighter. Necklaces, amulets, and other charms related to the warrior's supernatural guardian or vision spirit.

War paint

War paint was applied to the face and body in designs that were usually personal, though old wounds might be highlighted. Warriors also painted designs on their horses—a streak of lightning, for example, was believed to encourage a horse to run faster.

Amulet

An ornamental charm with a magic symbol or spell on it.

Warrior Societies

Among the Plains peoples, it was traditional for warriors to belong to special societies. Some tribes had separate, graded societies for warriors of similar age and experience. Others had ungraded societies for warriors of all ages.

Warriors in graded societies moved upward through the various societies. Blackfoot warriors, for example, began their careers in the Pigeon society, then moved up through the ranks to the Mosquitoes, the Braves, the Crazy Dogs, and finally to the most senior society, the Kit Foxes (also called the Tails or the Horns by some Blackfoot groups).

Buying membership

To move up to the next society, a warrior had to buy his membership. He did this by offering gifts to a member of that society who was himself seeking promotion. In return for his gifts, the warrior was given a special costume to wear and initiated in a special ceremony. Groups of warriors often moved up together from one society to the next. At the end of their careers, they gave up their membership in the most senior society and retired as active warriors.

Intense rivalry

With ungraded societies, there was no promotion from one to another since all were equal. Strong rivalries developed between ungraded warrior societies, each wanting to prove they were the bravest. The Lumpwood and Fox societies of the Crow, for example, competed fiercely with each other. Members of these societies used to kidnap each other's wives to discredit the rival society. The members would also try to outdo each other in feats of bravery and daring. During warfare, the warriors of the Crow societies would challenge one another to see who would gain the most important war honors.

Initiated
Gaining membership of a society through taking part in a special ritual.

Curriculum Context

When comparing Native American and European social organization, students could examine the different attitudes toward warfare between Plains warrior societies and the U.S. Army.

Codes and privileges

All warrior societies, whether graded or ungraded, expected their members to follow a strict code of behavior. Any member who did not do so faced being expelled from the society—a dishonorable fate for a Native American warrior.

Officers in societies enjoyed special privileges but were expected to show extra courage in return. As badges of office, and therefore of their success as warriors, they wore special items of clothing or carried banners or lances. They were marked men on the battlefield, since killing a senior warrior or touching him with a special stick—counting coup—was a prized war honor.

Curriculum Context

A study of Plains warrior societies will provide evidence of many common elements but also of local differences.

Extreme bravery

Some elite societies demanded extreme bravery from all their members. Members of No Flight societies, for example, wore long sashes into battle. Picking the most dangerous spots on the battlefield, they staked their sashes to the ground before fighting. They were not allowed to move unless a fellow member released their sash. Any No Flight warrior who retreated too soon faced permanent disgrace. No Flight societies included the Cheyenne Dog Soldiers and the Kaitsenko of the Kiowa. The Kaitsenko had only 10 members at any one time, and warriors invited to join were not allowed to refuse. It was traditional among some No Flight societies that their members said and did the opposite of what was meant. For example, if their leader ordered them not to shoot, they shot; if he ordered them to move slowly, they ran as fast as they could.

Warriors

Warriors were key figures in many Native American societies. On the Great Plains and in the Woodlands and Southeast, warfare was a major part of life and becoming a warrior was how a man gained respect and recognition. Even peaceable peoples, such as the Hopi and Pima of the Southwest, needed warriors to defend them.

Successful warriors were always highly regarded and occupied exalted positions of honor and high status. Among some groups, including the Siouan-speaking tribes of the Plains, it was essential that a man demonstrated his bravery and gained war honors before he could even be considered as a leader, or chief, of his people. But this was balanced by the

A Seminole warrior, painted in the 1840s. The Seminole peoples of Florida were at war with the United States government for much of the first half of the 19th century and never surrendered.

requirement that he should not be overly aggressive and had also to demonstrate qualities of forgiveness and generosity. In this way, a warrior proved he had the courage to defend his people if necessary but also possessed the wisdom not to lead them heedlessly into danger.

Curriculum Context

Students can compare Native American attitudes to war, and the values and beliefs of their warriors, with those of European armies in North America.

Unlike European armies, Native American war parties did not fight battles over land or property, and sometimes even killing an enemy was of little importance. The Plains tribes valued bravery above all else and graded their war honors according to how dangerous they were. Snatching a rifle from an enemy's hand, for example, was of greater risk than shooting an enemy from far away. So grabbing the gun was the higher war honor, even though the warrior did not kill the enemy in the process.

One of the most highly prized war honors was the act called counting coup. To count coup, a warrior had to touch a live enemy with his hand or with a special coup stick and escape unharmed, leaving the enemy also uninjured. As was the case with other war honors, the more senior the enemy touched, the more credit the warrior gained—but the coup could not be claimed unless another warrior saw it take place.

Apprentice warriors

Training to be a warrior began at an early age. A boy's grandfather made him his first bow and arrows when he was about five years old. He also started to teach him to follow animal and moccasin tracks and to move silently along trails. A boy was already highly skilled and a proficient hunter when he joined his first war party at about 14 years old. He did not fight on this occasion but carried water and spare moccasins for the full-fledged warriors and watched how the party was organized. In order to test him, he was made to do menial and tiring work, such as fetching water all night and then marching with the war party all the following day. If he proved a willing learner, he was given more responsible tasks until finally he was allowed to take part in a raid.

Guardian spirits

Despite their obvious bravery, Native American warriors did not ride into battle unprotected. Instead, they sought visions in which an animal spirit appeared and gave them power over their enemies. If a warrior dreamed of a hawk, for example, he would believe the power of the hawk to strike swiftly would help him in battle. Similarly, if he dreamed of a mouse, he would be able to creep silently and undetected into the lodges of his enemies while they were sleeping.

Once he discovered his guardian animal spirit, the warrior painted his shield and war costume with its likeness. He might also decorate his shield with parts of his guardian's body, such as a bear's claw or an eagle's feathers. Some warriors of the Southeast even tattooed their faces and bodies with marks that represented their guardian animal spirits.

The stealthy Apache

The Apache of the Southwest had a different attitude to warfare from that of the Plains peoples. Although just as fearless as Plains warriors, and with a reputation for being perhaps the best guerrilla fighters in North America, the Apache did not respect acts of reckless daring such as counting coup. They used stealth when they raided other Native Americans for horses or when they went to war to avenge Apache killed by their enemies. They also planned carefully before they attacked and underwent long rituals conducted by a shaman to guarantee success.

Guerrilla
Military techniques by which small bands of warriors carry out a campaign of harassment against the enemy.

Because Apache warriors valued life and killed only when provoked, an Apache warrior who had killed any of the enemy needed to be ritually purified after a battle before he could go back to everyday life among his people.

Glossary

Acadia The French name for their lands in northeastern North America that included parts of eastern Quebec, New Brunswick, Nova Scotia, Prince Edward Island, and New England.

American Indian Religious Freedom Act This law (1978) pledged to protect and preserve the traditional religious rights of Native Americans and stopped other laws interfering with their religious practices.

Atlatl A spear thrower consisting of a rod or board with a hook or thong at the back to hold the spear.

Bat Cave A complex of rock shelters in New Mexico, which were occupied for about 10,000 years and contained corn kernels more than 3,000 years old.

Bureau of Indian Affairs A U.S. federal government agency, formed in 1824, that administers land held in trust by the United States for Native Americans.

Clan A social unit consisting of a number of households or families with a common ancestor.

Fort Laramie Treaty A treaty signed in 1868 at Fort Laramie, Wyoming, between the United States and the Sioux and Arapaho.

French and Indian War A war (1754–1763) fought between Britain and France and their respective native allies for colonial supremacy in North America. British victory was confirmed in the Treaty of Paris in 1763.

Ghost Dance A Native American religious movement of the late 19th century that involved the performance of a ritual dance, which, it was believed, would bring an end to the westward expansion of whites and restore land and traditional tribal life to Native Americans.

Guardian spirit Some Native Americans formed a relationship with a spirit, usually of an animal, that was their spiritual guide and protector. All animals also had a guardian spirit. Hunters had to pray to the guardian spirits of the animals they killed so that they did not offend them.

Hudson's Bay Company A trading company set up in 1670 in the Hudson Bay area of North America. It controlled the fur trade in the region for centuries.

Indian Removal Act A federal law signed by President Andrew Jackson in 1830 to authorize the removal of Native Americans from their lands in the east and their resettlement in the west.

Indian Territory Land mainly in present-day Oklahoma set aside in 1834 for Native Americans who had been forced to leave their homelands. The Indian Territory was dissolved when Oklahoma became a state in 1907.

Initiated Gaining membership of a society through taking part in a special ritual.

Iroquois League of Nations A league of northeastern native peoples. These peoples were the Mohawk, Oneida, Onondaga, Cayuga, and Seneca, and later, the Tuscarora.

Kachinas Spirit beings in the religion of Pueblo cultures. Dolls representing kachinas are carved and given to children to educate them. In ceremonial dances, people dress as kachinas.

Massachusetts Bay Colony A colony consisting of a group of settlements of English people called Puritans, who had fled religious persecution in England. The colony had its own laws and by 1636 had more than 24 settlements.

Medicine Lodge Treaty A set of three separate treaties signed in 1867 at Medicine Lodge Creek, Kansas, between the U.S federal government and the Kiowa, Comanche, Plains Apache, Southern Cheyenne, and Arapaho peoples. The treaties involved the surrender of tribal homelands in exchange for reservations in the Indian Territory.

Midewiwin A medicine society in the Ojibway tribe. Its members perform curing rituals, using healing herbs and mysticism to promote physical and spiritual well-being.

Moccasins Shoes made of one piece of deerskin or soft leather, stitched together.

Moiety One of the two groups into which many Native American tribes were divided. Each was often composed of related clans, and marriage to someone of the same moiety was usually forbidden.

New England The region of the United States first settled by the English from 1620. It includes Maine, New Hampshire, Vermont, Massachusetts, Rhode Island, and Connecticut.

New France The area of North America colonized by France up to 1763. This territory was eventually divided into five colonies: Canada, Acadia, Hudson Bay, Newfoundland, and Louisiana.

Pueblo Rebellion An uprising of Pueblo peoples against Spanish colonization in August 1680. Many Spanish settlers and Franciscan priests were killed, and the Spanish fled from the city of Santa Fe.

Reservation An area of land set aside for a specific tribe, governed by a tribal council and with its own laws. Its contact with the federal government is through the Bureau of Indian Affairs.

Royal Proclamation This British order of King George III in 1763 set aside the Indian Reserve, mainly made up of land in Louisiana and Canada taken from the French, for use by Native Americans.

Rupert's Land The vast area of modern-day Canada from which rivers drain into Hudson Bay. It was owned by the Hudson's Bay Company from 1670 to 1870.

Scalp To remove hair and skin from the head of an enemy.

Shaman A person with special powers to access the spirit world and an ability to use magic to heal the sick and control events.

Sun Dance An important ceremony practiced by Plains peoples to celebrate the renewal of nature.

Tepee A cone-shaped tent built with a pole framework and traditionally covered with animal skins.

Totem poles Sculptures carved from large trees by tribes of the Northwest Coast. The designs illustrate legends or important events, clan lineages, or shamanic powers.

Umiak A large boat, similar in construction to a kayak, made for use in Arctic coastal areas by indigenous peoples. It can hold around 20 people and is used to transport people and their possessions and for hunting whales and walrus.

Wigwam The Eastern name for a domed dwelling consisting of a single room, formed on a frame of arched poles and covered with a roofing material such as birchbark, grass, or hides.

Further Research

BOOKS

Brown, Dee. *Bury My Heart at Wounded Knee: An Indian History of the American West*. Holt Paperbacks, 2007.

Cheewa, James. *Modoc: The Tribe That Wouldn't Die*. Naturegraph Publishers, 2008.

Cohen, Ken. *Honoring the Medicine: The Essential Guide to Native American Healing*. Ballantyne Books, 2006.

Deloria, Vine, and David E. Wilkins. *Tribes, Treaties, and Constitutional Tribulations*. University of Texas Press, 2000.

Dowd, Gregory Evans. *War Under Heaven: Pontiac, the Indian Nations, and the British Empire*. Johns Hopkins University Press, 2004.

Johansen, Bruce E. *The Native Peoples of North America: A History*. Rutgers University Press, 2006.

Kavasch, E. Barry. *Native Harvests: American Indian Wild Foods and Recipes*. Dover Publications, 2005.

Montgomery, David. *Native American Crafts and Skills: A Fully Illustrated Guide to Wilderness Living and Survival*. Lyons Press, 2008.

Nabokov, Peter. *Native American Testimony*. Penguin, 1999.

National Museum of the American Indian, George Horse Capture, and Emil Her Many Horses. *Song for the Horse Nation: Horses in Native American Cultures*. Fulcrum Publishing, 2006.

Nerburn, Kent. *Chief Joseph & the Flight of the Nez Perce: The Untold Story of an American Tragedy*. HarperOne, 2006.

Ostler, Jeffrey. *The Plains Sioux and U.S. Colonialism from Lewis and Clark to Wounded Knee*. Cambridge University Press, 2004.

Patent, Dorothy Hinshaw. *The Buffalo and the Indians: A Shared Destiny*. Clarion Books, 2006.

Paterek, Josephine. *Encyclopedia of American Indian Costume*. W. W. Norton & Company, 1996.

Pritzker, Barry M., ed. *A Native American Encyclopedia: History, Culture & Peoples*. Oxford University Press, USA, 2000.

Roberts, David. *Once They Moved Like the Wind: Cochise, Geronimo, and the Apache Wars*. Touchstone, 2005.

Starkey, Armstrong. *European and Native American Warfare. 1675–1815*. University of Oklahoma Press, 1998.

Utley, Robert M., and Wilcomb E. Washburn. *Indian Wars*. Mariner Books, 2002.

Yenne, Bill. *Indian Wars: The Campaign for the American West*. Westholme Publishing, 2008.

INTERNET RESOURCES

DesertUSA. This Guide to the American Southwest and Desert Regions has a section on peoples and cultures with many articles on Native Americans, ancient peoples, rock art, and Spanish explorers and missionaries.
www.desertusa.com

Indian Pueblo Cultural Center. Information on the 19 Pueblo peoples of New Mexico, their history, and arts and crafts.
www.indianpueblo.org

National Museum of the American Indian. The Smithsonian Institution's National Museum of the American Indian website. The site provides information about the museum's collections as well as educational resources for students about the history and culture of Native Americans.
www.nmai.si.edu/

Native American History. Site from the University of Washington with links to information on all aspects of Native American history.
www.lib.washington.edu/subject/history/tm/native.html

NativeAmericans.com. A comprehensive site with information and links about all aspects of Native American culture and history, including online biographies, extensive bibliographies, and information about the history and culture of Native American groups.
www.nativeamericans.com

Native Americans Documents Project. Provides access to documents relating to Native American history, including federal Indian policy and the Dawes General Allotment Act.
www2.csusm.edu/nadp/

NorthWestCoast Indians. Photos and descriptions of Northwest Coast historical artifacts.
www.northwestcoastindian.com

Smithsonian: American Indian History and Culture. A Smithsonian Institution website, with information about all aspects of Native American history and culture.
www.si.edu/Encyclopedia_SI/History_and_Culture/AmericanIndian_History.htm

Index